VALUING THE COST OF SMOKING

Studies in Risk and Uncertainty

edited by
W. Kip Viscusi
Harvard Law School
Cambridge, MA 02138

Previously published books in the series:

Luken, R.: ENVIRONMENTAL REGULATION:
TECHNOLOGY, AMBIENT AND BENEFITS-BASED APPROACHES
Shubik, M.: RISK, ORGANIZATIONS AND SOCIETY
Edwards, W.: UTILITY THEORIES: MEASUREMENTS AND APPLICATIONS
Martin, W.: ENVIRONMENTAL ECONOMICS AND THE MINING INDUSTRY
Kunreuther, H. and Easterling, D.:
THE DILEMMA OF A SITING OF HIGH-LEVEL NUCLEAR WASTE REPOSITORY
Kniesner, T. and Leeth, J.: SIMULATING WORKPLACE SAFETY POLICY
Christe, N.G.S. and Soguel, N.C.
CONTINGENT VALUATION, TRANSPORT SAFETY
Battigalli, P., Montesano, A. and Panunzi, F.:
DECISIONS, GAMES AND MARKETS
Freeman, P. and Kunreuther, H.:
MANAGING ENVIRONMENTAL RISK THROUGH INSURANCE
Kopp, R.J., Pommerehne, W.W. and Schwarz, N.:
DETERMINING THE VALUE OF NON-MARKETED GOODS
Bishop, R.C. and Romano, D.:
ENVIRONMENTAL RESOURCE VALUATION: APPLICATIONS OF THE CONTINGENT VALUATION METHOD IN ITALY
Levy, Haim:
STOCHASTIC DOMINANCE: INVESTMENT DECISION MAKING UNDER UNCERTAINTY

VALUING THE COST OF SMOKING
ASSESSMENT METHODS, RISK PERCEPTION AND POLICY OPTIONS

EDITED BY CLAUDE JEANRENAUD AND NILS SOGUEL

SPRINGER SCIENCE+BUSINESS MEDIA, LLC

Library of Congress Cataloging-in-Publication Data

Valuing the cost of smoking : assessment methods, risk perception, and policy options / edited by Claude Jeanrenaud and Nils Soguel.
p. cm. -- (Studies in risk and uncertainty)
"This volume is the outcome of a conference held in Lausanne, Switzerland in August 1998"--Introd.
Includes bibliographical references and index.
ISBN 978-94-010-5898-8 ISBN 978-94-011-4415-5 (eBook)
DOI 10.1007/978-94-011-4415-5
1. Smoking--Costs. 2. Smoking--Health aspects--Costs. 3. Smoking--Economic aspects. I. Jeanrenaud, Claude. II. Soguel, Nils C. III. Series.
HV5735.V35 1999
338.4'36797--dc21 99-40852
CIP

Originally published by Kluwer Academic Publishers in 1999
Softcover reprint of the hardcover 1st edition 1999

Printed on acid-free paper.

This printing is a digital duplication of the original edition.

TABLE OF CONTENTS

COUNTRY STUDIES

RISK PERCEPTION, DEMAND AND TAXATION

CONTRIBUTORS

JAN J. BARENDREGT	*Institute for Medical Technology Assessment, Erasmus University, Netherlands*
LUC BONNEUX	*Institute for Medical Technology Assessment, Erasmus University, Netherlands*
FRANK CHALOUPKA	*Department of Economics, University of Illinois at Chicago, U.S.A.*
DAVID COLLINS	*School of Health Services Management, University of New South Wales, Australia*
ANDREAS FREI	*HealthEcon AG, Basel, Switzerland*
JONI HERSCH	*Harvard Law School, U.S.A.*
CLAUDE JEANRENAUD	*Institut de recherches économiques et régionales, Université de Neuchâtel, Switzerland*
PER-OLOV JOHANSSON	*Centre for Health Economics, Department of Economics, Stockholm School of Economics, Sweden*
MARC A. KOOPMANSCHAP	*Institute for Medical Technology Assessment, Erasmus University, Netherlands*

HELEN LAPSLEY	*School of Health Services Management, University of New South Wales, Australia*
ANIL MARKANDYA	*School of Social Sciences, University of Bath, United Kingdom*
SANDRA NOCERA	*Volkswirtschaftliches Institut der Universität Bern, Switzerland*
MARKKU PEKURINEN	*Health Services Research Ltd, Helsinki Finland*
FRANCE PRIEZ	*Institut de recherches économiques et régionales, Université de Neuchâtel, Switzerland*
DOROTHY P. RICE	*University of California, U.S.A.*
ERIC SINGLE	*University of Toronto, Canada*
NILS SOGUEL	*IDHEAP, Université de Lausanne, Switzerland*
PAUL J. VAN DER MAAS	*Institute for Medical Technology Assessment, Erasmus University, Netherlands*
W. KIP VISCUSI	*Harvard Law School, U.S.A.*
SARINO VITALE	*Institut de recherches économiques et régionales, Université de Neuchâtel, Switzerland*
PETER ZWEIFEL	*Sozialökonomisches Seminar der Universität Zürich, Switzerland*

INTRODUCTION

CLAUDE JEANRENAUD
NILS SOGUEL

Smoking is a very common habit all over the world. The prevalence rate ranges from 20% - 40% in industrialised countries, and is dramatically increasing in the developing world. Smoking is risky and there is ample scientific evidence to support this statement. We know that smoking is a major cause of disease and premature death, in view of the fact that 3 million people die each year worldwide as a result of their smoking habit. Twenty years ago, the U.S. Surgeon General identified smoking as the single most important cause of morbidity and premature death (USDHEW, 1979). Tobacco consumption reduces life expectancy vastly. Epidemiological research shows that people who have died from a smoking-related disease would, on average, have lived for an additional 15 years had they not been smokers (Warner, 1987).

The economic analysis of tobacco consumption is a complex and challenging issue, which entails addressing many different questions. What is the economic burden of smoking and do smokers "pay their way"? How do individuals perceive their own health risks? What is the effect of the addicting properties of nicotine on the behaviour of a rational, utility-maximizing individual? Lastly, what is the most effective way to discourage tobacco consumption? In this context, the assessment of the social burden of smoking using a cost-of-illness framework has played a central role since the beginning of the seventies. Interest in this type of study has grown even more in the wake of the lawsuits brought by American states against the tobacco companies with the aim of recovering excessive medical costs resulting from smoking-related diseases. Economists argue that there is no need for government intervention on condition that smokers receive accurate information about the health hazards – including the risk of addiction – and that they bear all the costs of smoking themselves. Economists agree on this last point: smokers bear most if not all of the economic costs of tobacco consumption. Moreover, a better understanding of the determinants of smoking and of the public perception of the risks of smoking could help decision-makers to improve the design of tobacco control policies.

The purpose of this publication is to review the various methods used to value the adverse health outcomes of smoking, from the standard human capital approach to the new preference-based methods, with which intangibles can be assessed. This raises some controversial questions, such as, for example, whether smokers really do generate extra costs for the health system – in the U.S. the lifetime medical costs of smokers apparently exceed those of non-smokers by more than $6,000 (USDHHS, 1992) – or whether these costs are offset, in part or entirely, by the shorter life span of smokers. This publication should also help understand better the behaviour of smokers as well as the factors which determine the demand for cigarettes. We learn how a rational person would behave regarding tobacco consumption, and how she or he would respond to public policy incentives, such as taxes or the dissemination of information about the health hazards of smoking. Special attention is devoted to the potential failure of markets, which constitutes the rationale for government action. A key question in this context is whether smokers correctly perceive the risks they face. In order to incite smokers to change their behaviour, economists prefer policy instruments, which rely on market forces, such as an increase in the price of cigarettes. Lastly, the publication contains a review of the scientific evidence regarding the effectiveness of taxes in reducing tobacco use.

This volume is the outcome of the conference held in Lausanne (Switzerland) in August 1998. It was organised to mark the completion of a two-year research programme funded by the Swiss Federal Office of Public Health and devoted to the social cost of smoking in Switzerland, (Vitale *et al.*, 1998). This publication introduces the reader to the various aspects of the economics of tobacco consumption: the cost of smoking-related diseases, the methodology applied to the assessment of medical costs, the reduction in economic output due to morbidity and mortality, the loss in quality of life, the economic rationale for government intervention, and lastly the choice of control policy instruments. Thus, the publication should interest professional economists, health policy analysts and decision-makers at the federal, state and local level.

CONCEPTS AND METHODS

The first part of this volume discusses the conceptual framework and the methods used to assess the economic cost of the adverse health effects of smoking. Some recent controversies concerning the proper way of assessing the social burden of smoking are also highlighted. *Dorothy Rice* has conducted some seminal work on the development of the cost-of-illness methodology and the assessment of the adverse effects of substance abuse. In the first paper, she presents the analytical foundation of the cost-of-illness approach and shows how the method has evolved from the first attempts to measure the cost of smoking in the early seventies to the most recent work by Bartlett *et al.* (1994) and Miller *et al.* (1998); she also points out some unanswered questions. *David Collins and Helen Lapsley* propose an alternative approach to the traditional human capital methodology. The so-called demographic approach is applied to assess the economic impact of smoking in Australia. The novelty of this approach is that it does not require future lifetime earnings to be discounted. In fact, it compares the actual population by size and structure with the hypothetical "non-smoking" population during the year of calculation. The estimate of the savings in health expenditure and in consumption due to the premature death of smokers is made much easier, but the method can only be applied where comprehensive epidemiological data is available. The *Marc Koopmanschap* paper discusses the controversial question of whether the human capital provides an accurate estimate of the indirect costs of illness. The actual loss of production for society may be much smaller than the value obtained with the human capital approach. According to the argument of the advocates of the so-called friction cost method, the sick person can be replaced – in the case of short-term incapacity by other employees working in the same company, and in the case of long-term absences by unemployed individuals. Using the friction cost method leads to much lower costs estimates. *Per-Olov Johansson* was asked to respond to the question whether we should apply the contingent valuation method or QALYs to assess the adverse health effects of smoking. Market data – the price of cigarettes – does not provide sufficient information to calculate the value of a statistical life. Thus, there is a role for contingent valuation in cost assessment if the method is used carefully. The implementation of a CV survey to value the consequences of smoking is difficult considering the complexity of the adverse outcomes. Finally, the author wonders if both methods could be applied simultaneously, the CV survey being used to place a monetary value on QALYs. *Jan Barendregt, Luc Bonneux and Paul van der Maas* examine the controversial issue of whether the lifetime medical costs of a smoker exceed those of a non-smoker as suggested by the U.S. Surgeon General in

1992 (USDHHS, 1992). However we know that smokers have a shorter life expectancy, and thus die at a younger age on the average than non-smokers. The authors conclude that the lifetime costs are higher for a statistical non-smoker, even if the annual medical costs of smokers are larger at all ages, the reason being the shorter life span of smokers. Finally, they assess the consequences for medical costs of a policy that would change smoking prevalence. All the previous contributions show that many discussions are still ongoing regarding the way of assessing the economic cost of smoking. At the same time attempts are being made to find a consensus about the most appropriate valuation model. *Eric Single* has played a leading role in the development of a set of guidelines for the estimation of the cost of substance abuse. The guidelines cover the purpose of cost estimates, the analytical framework including the different cost categories to be assessed, and the methodological issues. The author presents the findings of a study of substance abuse in Canada based on these guidelines.

COUNTRY STUDIES

The second part of this volume contains two case studies conducted in Finland and in Switzerland. These studies illustrate how the adverse outcomes of smoking have been valued in money terms. Both were carried out to provide policy makers with a recent estimate of the economic burden of smoking, and to help them design and promote smoking-control policies and programs. *Markku Pekurinen* has assessed the economic consequences of smoking in Finland in 1995, and compares this result with the outcome of an earlier study (Pekurinen, 1991). The aim of these studies was to provide the Finnish government with information allowing it to decide about the benefits of public intervention on the tobacco market. The author concludes that smokers as a group pay for the external costs they impose on non-smokers. *France Priez, Claude Jeanrenaud, Sarino Vitale and Andreas Frei* have assessed the social cost of smoking in Switzerland in 1995. The novelty of the approach lies in the value assigned to the non-marketable consequences of smoking, such as suffering, loss in quality of life, and reduced life expectancy. Production losses are estimated using the standard human capital approach, whereas the intangible cost estimate relies on the willingness-to-pay approach. The study shows that the intangible costs represent a higher burden than the value of the production lost. It is interesting to note that smokers in Switzerland seem to have made an accurate use of the information given to them about the potential risks of smoking. Their perception of the relative risks of contracting lung cancer is fairly close to those established by scientific evidence. The comment made by *Sandra Nocera* stresses the policy relevance of the outcome of cost-of-illness studies. The mere existence of a high social cost does not mean that governmental action is needed. Only when the market fails as a consequence of externalities, risk misperception or, in some circumstances, addiction should the state intervene.

RISK PERCEPTION, DEMAND AND GOVERNMENTAL ACTION

The third part of the volume consists of four papers and deals with smokers' behavior, rationality in smoking decisions, risk perception, the smoking preference by gender, the rationale of government action, and the choice of policy approach to tobacco control. *W. Kip Viscusi* – the author of numerous publications on health and safety risks (Viscusi, 1992) – shows that smokers do not have an accurate perception of the health risk they face. They tend to greatly over-assess the health risks of smoking as compared with scientific evidence, despite the widespread public information efforts undertaken in the last 30 years. The federal government provides data on the incidence of smoking-related diseases, instead of informing smokers about the probability of specific health outcomes, which could explain part of the risk misperception. The message that smoking is a risky activity seems to be well understood. Therefore, the government should devise new strategies, e.g. informing people of the hazard of alternative cigarette designs. These conclusions give rise to a comment by *Peter Zweifel*, whose message underlines some surprising policy implications of Viscusi's findings. Filling the information gap, i.e. providing smokers with accurate information about the probability of adverse health effects, would increase tobacco consumption. Zweifel's comment focuses on tobacco policy as a tool to internalize the external costs of smoking using a partial equilibrium model. A tax on tobacco combined with better information given to smokers would have some unexpected consequences, such as a higher burden for the community. Thus, alternative policy approaches deserve to be considered. Using a stochastic lifetime consumption model, *Anil Markandya* examines the tobacco consumption of a rational individual whose behavior is aimed at maximizing expected utility. The model helps us to understand how a rational individual would act regarding tobacco consumption, and how she or he would respond to policy incentives such as taxes or information campaigns.

The contribution by *Joni Hersch* discusses the health outcomes of smoking using a gender perspective. The author considers the various individual characteristics as determinants of smoking behavior. Because the influence of these factors differs by gender, women could respond differently to public policies aimed at reducing smoking. The analysis of the data of a national population survey suggests that the usual instruments would deter both women and men from smoking, but that the outcome could differ by gender. *Frank Chaloupka* reviews scientific evidence from the literature to see how effective taxes are in reducing tobacco consumption and smoking prevalence. He shows that the law of diminishing demand remains valid for cigarettes, in spite of the addictive nature of cigarette consumption. A key finding from recent studies regarding the price-demand relation indicates that the long-term effect of a higher price of cigarettes is much stronger than the short-term effect. The review also shows that a tax increase would not only reduce the consumption of current smokers, but would also lower the prevalence of smoking.

REFERENCES

Pekurinen M. (1991), *Economic Aspects of Smoking. Is there a case for government intervention in Finland?,* Research Reports 16/1991, National Agency for Welfare and Health, Helsinki.

U.S. Department of Health, Education and Welfare (1979), *Smoking and Health. A Report of the Surgeon General*, Office on Smoking and Health, Public Health Service, Rockville, pp. I 10-28.

U.S. Department of Health and Human Services (1992), *Smoking and Health in the Americas: a 1992 Report of the Surgeon General*, in collaboration with the Pan American Health Organization, DHHS publication No. (CDC) 92-8419.

Viscusi W.K. (1992), *Smoking: Making the Risky Decision*, Oxford University Press, Oxford.

Vitale S., Priez F. and Jeanrenaud C. (1998), *Le coût social de la consommation de tabac en Suisse*, rapport final, Institut de recherches économiques et régionales, Neuchâtel.

Warner K. (1998), "The Economics of Tobacco and Health: an Overview", in Abedian I. and van der Merwe R. (Eds.), *The Economics of Tobacco Control: Towards an optimal policy mix*, Applied Fiscal Research Centre, University of Cape Town.

CONCEPTS AND METHODS

1

MEASUREMENT OF THE ECONOMIC COSTS OF SMOKING IN THE UNITED STATES: AN HISTORICAL REVIEW

DOROTHY P. RICE

The health hazards of smoking have been well documented (CDC, 1989). Cigarette smoking has been and continues to be a major cause of illness, disability, premature death, and productivity losses in the United States and throughout the world. Estimates of the cost of smoking translate the adverse health effects of smoking into monetary terms, the universal language of decision-makers and those in the policy arena. This paper describes the health economic concepts and alternative economic approaches used in estimating smoking costs and reviews the published studies on national smoking cost estimates in the United States, focusing on the methodological changes, new data sources, and advancements made over the years in these areas.

HEALTH ECONOMIC CONCEPTS

Underlying the cost of smoking are several conceptual and methodological health economic issues that are summarized below.

Prevalence and incidence-based approaches

Two approaches to estimating the cost of smoking have been employed in the past: prevalence-based and incidence-based. Prevalence-based costs estimate the direct and indirect economic burden incurred in a period of time (the base period) as a result of the prevalence of disease, a period most often a year. Included are the costs of current and past smoking. Prevalence-based costs measure the value of resources used or lost during a specified period of time, regardless of the time of disease onset. Incidence-based costs represent the lifetime costs resulting from a disease or illness. In the aggregate, incidence-based costs refer to the total lifetime costs of all cases with onset of disease in a given base year.

The approach used depends on the purpose of the analysis. If the results are to be used for cost control, then prevalence-based costing is appropriate. It identifies the major components of current expenditures and forgone resources and identifies possible targets for economy. In cost of smoking studies, the prevalence approach has been used to define the annual impact of cigarette smoking on the delivery and financing of health services, to study the likely impact of interventions such as increases in cigarette taxes, and to guide health policy and planning relative to smoking control initiatives. If the analysis is aimed at making decisions about which treatment or research strategy to implement, then the incidence-based approach is more appropriate because its provides the basis for predictions about the likely savings from programs that reduce incidence or improve outcomes. In cost of smoking studies, incidence-based costing reveals the relative costs of ever-smokers versus nonsmokers over their lifetimes, providing a basis for assessing the impact of becoming a smoker (Hodgson, 1992).

Both approaches have been used in cost of smoking studies. This paper will review the methods, data sources, and results of both types of studies.

Components of costs

The adverse health effects of smoking impose an enormous burden on society, encompassing the cost associated with the use of medical resources and the value of productivity lost due to illness and premature death. Cost of smoking studies generally include two major components: direct and indirect costs. Direct costs include expenditures for hospital and nursing home care, physician and other professional services, and medications. Indirect costs include morbidity and mortality costs. Morbidity costs are the value of productivity lost by persons unable to perform their usual activities or unable to perform them at full effectiveness due to smoking-related illness. Mortality costs are productivity losses due to premature death resulting from smoking-attributable disease. Lost productivity is calculated as the present discounted value of future market earnings plus an imputed value for housekeeping services.

Human capital approach

The human capital approach is used in estimating the indirect costs. In the human capital approach, a person is seen as producing a stream of output that is valued at market earnings and the value of life is the discounted future earnings stream. Morbidity and mortality destroy labour, a valuable economic resource, by causing persons to lose time and effectiveness from work and other productive activities, forcing them out of the labour force, reducing household production or bringing about premature death. Disease thus creates an undeniable loss to individuals and society, and it is this loss that the human capital approach attempts to measure.

REVIEW OF PREVALENCE-BASED STUDIES

Table I lists the national prevalence-based studies in the United States since the late 1960's and the total costs, by type of cost, for each study. Omitted from this review are studies of Medicaid smoking costs (Miller *et al.* 1998a) and studies of cost of smoking for specific states (Rice and Max, 1992). Following the table is a brief review of the methodology and sources of data for each study.

Table I *Prevalence-based smoking cost studies, by type of cost, United States*

		Type of Cost ($ Billions, U.S.)			
Study	**Study Year**	**Total**	**Direct**	**Morbidity**	**Mortality**
Hedrick (1971)	1966	$ 5.3	$ 1.1	-	$ 4.2[1]
Kristein (1977)	1975	20.3	5.2	$ 3.1	12.0[2]
Luce & Schweitzer (1978)	1976	27.3	8.2	6.2	12.9[3]
Rice *et al.* (1986)	1980	38.6	14.4	7.4	16.8[3]
Rice *et al.* (1986)	1984	53.7	23.3	9.3	21.1[3]
PHS (1990)	1985	52.3	23.7	10.2	18.4[4]
OTA (1985)	1985	65.0	22.0	-	43.0[1]
OTA (1993)	1990	68.0	20.8	6.9	40.3[3]
Bartlett *et al.* (1994)	1987	-	21.9	-	-
Bartlett *et al.* (1994)	1993	-	50.0	-	-
Miller *et al.* (1998b)	1993	-	72.7	-	-

[1] Discount rate not stated. [2] Discounted at 10%. [3] Discounted at 4%. [4] Discounted at 6%.

Hedrick (1971) study

One of the earliest prevalence-based studies published in the United States was by Hedrick (1971) in which he projected 1966 costs, obtained from a Canadian study, to the United States (Canadian Department of National Health and Welfare, 1967). Total costs of four diseases (lung cancer, coronary heart disease, chronic bronchitis, and emphysema) were estimated according to the methodology for estimating costs of illness by diagnosis developed by Rice (1966). An adjustment factor of 1.5 was applied to the cost of four diseases to extrapolate to all diseases. Smoking attributable percentages were obtained from the mortality ratios of a major prospective study (Hammond, 1966). After adding estimates of the morbidity costs and fires, the total in Canada amounted to $526.5 million. A multiplier of 10 was used to adjust Canadian costs to United States costs, $5.3 billion, based on the relationship of GNP between the United States and Canada. The discount rate (if used) for mortality costs is not reported.

Kristein (1977) study

This study estimated direct and indirect costs of heavy smoking at \$20.3 billion in 1975. Direct costs were based on an estimate of the total cost of hospital care and physicians' services, the number of heavy smokers, and the assumption that heavy cigarette smokers have a hospitalization rate 1.5 times that of nonsmokers. Morbidity costs were based on 77 million days lost from work due to smoking, at a rate of \$40 a day. The estimated 300,000 premature deaths were valued at \$10,000 per year for five years, using a discount rate of 10%.

Luce and Schweitzer (1978) study

The most commonly cited early study of the costs of smoking is the one prepared by Luce and Schweitzer. They used the Cooper and Rice (1976) direct and indirect 1972 cost estimates for three smoking-induced diseases and inflated them to 1975 dollars. Smoking-attributable fractions, taken from Boden (1976), were applied to the total costs as follows: neoplasms-20%, circulatory system-25%, and respiratory system-40%. Estimated costs of smoking-induced accidents due to fires were included in direct costs. Boden obtained these factors from physicians' opinions. Total costs of smoking amounted to \$27.3 billion in 1976, of which mortality costs were \$12.9 billion, discounted at 4%. The authors also estimated the direct and indirect costs of fires at \$413 million.

Office of Technology Assessment (1985) study

The Office of Technology Assessment (OTA) employed the method most commonly used in previous estimates of the costs of smoking. This method apportioned direct health care costs and indirect productivity costs using estimates of attributable risks for smoking-related mortality for three major diagnostic categories – cancers, circulatory diseases, and diseases of the respiratory system. The major assumption was that the proportion of costs attributable to smoking is equal to the proportion of deaths related to smoking in each disease category. The data for the 1980 costs of care for each major disease category by age and sex were from Hodgson and Kopstein (1984). The 1980 data were inflated to 1985 values by using the increase in personal health care expenditures.

OTA also estimated smoking-attributable mortality at 314,000 deaths in 1982. In 1985 dollars, the middle estimate for direct costs was \$22 billion;

indirect mortality costs were \$43 billion (discount rate not reported); and total costs were \$65 billion.

Rice *et al.* (1986) study

Most earlier studies estimated smoking-attributable direct costs based on proportions of deaths due to cigarette smoking or the relative risks of dying from smoking-related diseases by cause of death (mortality ratio approach). These proportions were applied to medical care utilization or to the estimated direct medical costs of the smoking-related diseases. The methodology for estimating the direct and indirect costs of smoking was further advanced by Rice and her colleagues in this 1986 study. Direct health care costs were calculated by a new method based on reported medical care utilization computed from the National Health Interview Survey (NHIS). Ratios of hospital days and physician visits for ever-smokers and never-smokers with neoplasms, circulatory diseases and respiratory diseases combined by age and sex were used to calculate attributable risk factors which were applied to total personal health care expenditures by type of care, age, and sex for these three disease categories.

Using a methodology parallel to that for direct costs, attributable risks for indirect morbidity losses due to smoking were derived from the NHIS for work-loss days among currently employed persons, bed-disability days among females whose usual activity is keeping house, and persons unable to work or keep house. These attributable risks were applied to the total morbidity costs for neoplasms, circulatory diseases, and respiratory diseases estimated by Rice *et al.* (1985) to obtain morbidity costs of smoking.

The methodology for estimating mortality costs was comparable to that for direct and morbidity costs. Attributable risks for deaths due to smoking were applied to total mortality costs of specific diseases estimated by Rice *et al.* (1985). Mortality costs, however, were estimated for 19 specific causes of death (270,000 deaths) attributed to smoking, discounted at 4% and 6%. The total estimate of smoking-attributable costs summed to \$38.6 billion: \$14.4 billion for direct costs, \$7.4 billion for morbidity costs, and \$16.8 billion for mortality costs at a 4% discount rate. These costs were updated to 1984 (see Table I) based on the percentage change in total personal health care expenditures reported by the Health Care Financing Administration (HCFA) for direct costs, and in the percentage change in average weekly earnings reported the Bureau of Labor Statistics for morbidity and mortality costs.

Public Health Service (1990) study

Subsequent to the publication of the Rice *et al.* (1986) study, a software program was developed by James Shultz *et al.* (1991) and provided to the States by the Centers for Disease Control and Prevention (CDC). This software program, Smoking-Attributable Mortality, Morbidity, and Economic Costs (SAMMEC), permits rapid calculations of death, years of potential life lost, direct health care costs, indirect mortality and morbidity costs. SAMMEC adapted the methodology used for national estimates of smoking-attributable costs developed by Rice *et al.* (1986) for use at State and local levels.

Using SAMMEC, the 1990 Public Health Service (PHS) study presented state-specific calculations for smoking-attributable mortality, years of potential life lost and economic costs in the United States. A total of 214,135 deaths in 1985 were attributed to smoking. The aggregate costs for 1985 for the United States were as follows: $ 23.7 billion for direct costs, $10.2 billion for morbidity costs, and $18.4 billion for mortality costs, at a 6% discount rate, for a total of $52.3 billion.

Office of Technology Assessment (1993) study

The Office of Technology Assessment (OTA) relied on SAMMEC for its estimates of the cost of smoking in the United States in 1990. Using SAMMEC 2.1 (CDC, 1992), a later version than that used by the Public Health Service, OTA estimated that 417,000 people died in 1990 as a consequence of smoking, almost twice the number estimated previously by the Public Health Service. Total costs amounted to $68 billion distributed as follows: $20.8 billion for direct costs, $6.9 billion for morbidity costs, and $40.3 billion for mortality costs, at a 4% discount rate.

Bartlett *et al.* (1994) study

One of the major criticisms of estimating the attributable risks of smoking based on medical utilization for smokers and nonsmokers has been that this approach does not control for sociodemographic and other differences that exist between smokers and nonsmokers, which may affect their medical care use and costs. To respond to this criticism, researchers at the University of California at Berkeley and at San Francisco employed a new and more sophisticated econometric approach and a new database to estimate the direct cost of smoking. They used data from the 1987 National Medical Expenditure Survey (NMES) conducted by the Agency for Health Care

Policy and Research (AHCPR). NMES is a population-based survey of a cohort of 35,000 persons in 14,000 households interviewed five times between February 1987 and May 1988. Respondents provided data about socio-demographic factors, health insurance coverage, use of medical care, and medical expenditures.

To estimate costs attributable to smoking, respondents were categorized as never smokers, former smokers with less than 15 years' exposure, former smokers with 15 or more years' exposure, and current smokers. First, the effect of smoking history on the presence of smoking-related medical conditions (i.e. heart disease, emphysema, arteriosclerosis, stroke, and cancer) was determined. Second, for each of the medical care expenditure categories (ambulatory care, prescription drugs, hospital care, and home health services), the probability of having any expenditures and the level of expenditures were estimated as a function of smoking, medical conditions, and health status. A total of 24 models (equations) were used – 2 gender groups, 3 age groups, and 4 types of medical expenditures. All models controlled for age, race/ethnicity, poverty status, marital status, educational level, medical insurance status, region of residence, safety belt non-use, and obesity. Data were weighted to project the estimated costs of smoking-attributable medical care in 1987 to the noninstitutionalized population in the United States. For 1993, the 1987 smoking-attributable fractions were applied to published national personal health expenditure data for 1993 reported by the Health Care Financing Administration (HCFA). Nursing home costs were estimated by applying the smoking-attributable fractions of hospital expenditures for persons aged 65 years and over to total nursing home expenditures reported by HCFA. Smoking-attributable medical expenditures in 1987 amounted to $21.9 billion in 1987 and $50 billion in 1993.

Miller *et al.* (1998b) study

This study represents a further refinement of the national model used in the Bartlett *et al.*, 1994 study that presented smoking-attributable medical expenditures for the nation and in the Miller *et al.* (1998a) study that presented state and national medical expenditures attributed to smoking. The smoking-attributable fractions (SAFs) of total state medical expenditures, by type of expenditure, were estimated using a revised national model based on the 1987 NMES data. In the latest study, two smoking history categories were defined: (a) current smokers and (b) a combined category of former smokers and respondents with missing information. Employing data from the 1993 state Behavioural Risk Factor Surveillance System (BRFSS), the national model was used to estimate SAFs for the 50 states, the District of Columbia, and the United States as a whole. These SAFs were applied to published state medical expenditures for 1993 (adjusted to exclude expenditures for persons under age 19), by type of expenditure, to estimate total state and national smoking-attributable expenditures (SAEs).

Smoking-attributable medical expenditures for the nation amounted to $72.7 billion. This estimate is 45% more than the $50 billion reported for the same year in Bartlett *et al.* (1994). This difference is due to several technical changes in the model. For example, the *MMWR* model used five different tobacco-related disease equations; the national model used in the more recent study has one tobacco-related disease equation. The *MMWR* study employed five expected linear disease probability models; the more recent study uses one probit probability model. These and other technical refinements resulted in higher SAFs and higher estimated SAEs.

REVIEW OF INCIDENCE-BASED STUDIES

Incidence-based studies that calculate the lifetime costs of smokers and nonsmokers have been the subject of some controversy. Some studies report that lifetime costs of smokers are higher than the lifetime costs of nonsmokers, while other studies report reverse results. Following is a brief review of these incidence-based studies:

Leu and Schaub (1983) and (1985) studies

Although these studies were conducted in Switzerland, they are included here because they are among the earliest incidence-based studies. The researchers estimated that total expected lifetime medical expenditures beginning at age 35 for Swiss males who do not smoke are higher than for smokers. They estimated that the average male smoker has 8% more physician visits and 10% more hospital days per year than never-smokers. They assumed that medical care utilization is related to smoking in the same way that mortality is related to smoking. Among Swiss males, the contribution of longer life expectancy to medical care expenditures for never-smokers outweighed the higher average annual expenditures for smokers. In their second study, Leu and Schaub analyzed the demand for medical care in Switzerland using an econometric model and concluded that smokers have fewer physician visits and slightly higher hospital days than never-smokers. They concluded again that smoking does not increase lifetime medical expenditures.

Oster *et al.* (1984) study

The estimates of discounted lifetime costs of smoking were obtained by combining age-sex-specific estimates of incidence-based costs of three smoking-related diseases (lung cancer, coronary heart disease, and emphysema) with estimates of increased likelihood of smokers developing these illnesses in each remaining year of life relative to nonsmokers. Estimates of the economic consequences of quitting based on these disease cost estimates and on estimates of ex-smokers' probability of future disease relative to continuing smokers are also reported. Both the estimates of the economic costs of smoking and the benefits of quitting were calculated separately for men and women between the ages of 35 and 79 who were light, moderate, and heavy cigarette smokers. Costs for a 40-year-old man, for example, ranged from \$20,000 for a smoker of less than one pack of cigarettes per day to over \$56,000 for a smoker of more than two packs of cigarettes per day. The economic benefits of quitting also were found to be sizeable for all groups of smokers.

Manning *et al.* (1989) study

This article estimates the lifetime discounted medical and other costs of smoking (and drinking) from the perspective of quantifying external costs, in which costs to others are estimated. The external costs come from collectively financed programs, including health insurance, pensions, sick leave, disability insurance and group life insurance, which are financed by taxes and premiums that do not differentiate between smokers and nonsmokers. Estimates were based on the RAND Corporation's Health Insurance Experiment (Newhouse, 1974) for persons under 60 years, and from the 1983 supplement to the National Health Interview Survey on health habits. The authors estimated differences in spending for medical care services and days lost from work between smokers and nonsmokers, controlling for health insurance coverage, age, sex, race, education, use of seat belts, family income, exercise, self-assessed measures of physical, mental, and general health, and family size. Their estimate was that medical care costs of smoking amounted to \$.26 per pack of cigarettes smoked in 1986 dollars discounted at 5%. They concluded that "On balance, smokers probably pay their way at the current level of excise taxes on cigarettes; but one may, nonetheless, wish to raise those taxes to reduce the number of adolescent smokers"(Manning *et al.*, 1989, p. 1604).

Lippiatt (1990) study

This study also reported that smoking lowers lifetime medical costs. The author deducted the additional medical costs incurred during the longer life of a nonsmoker from expected lifetime medical expenditures required to treat a smoker for three smoking-related diseases (lung cancer, coronary heart disease, and emphysema). The model used data on medical costs, life expectancy, cigarette price elasticity, and smoking demographics to estimate medical-cost and life-year impacts for any change in cigarette sales. The cost data were taken from Oster *et al.* (1984), who estimated lifetime costs of lung cancer, coronary heart disease, and emphysema. These lifetime costs were adjusted for the increase in other medical costs brought about by longer life expectancies. Hodgson (1992) states: "Although methodologically sound, lifetime medical costs of smoking were underestimated because the data employed both underestimate expenditures for the smoker's smoking-related diseases and overestimate medical costs during the longer life of the nonsmoker." (p. 82). Hodgson states further that by limiting the calculation to costs of lung cancer, coronary heart disease, and emphysema, Lippiatt omitted substantial morbidity, mortality, and health care utilization and severely underestimated lifetime medical costs of smoking.

Hodgson (1992) study

In his comprehensive study of cigarette smoking and lifetime medical expenditures, Hodgson found that smokers have higher lifetime medical expenditures than nonsmokers. Lifetime medical care expenditures were estimated for males and females in the United States who never smoked and for moderate and heavy smokers, including both former and current smokers. Medical care use, costs, and mortality experience of cross-sections of the population during each age interval were used to generate longitudinal profiles of costs from age 17 to death. The principal data sources were the National Health Interview Survey for hospital and physician services, the National Nursing Home Survey and the National Health and Nutrition Examination Survey Epidemiologic Follow-up Study for nursing home care, the American Cancer Society's Cancer Prevention Study II for mortality, and the National Medical Care Utilization and Expenditure Survey and Medicare data files for charges for medical care. Lifetime expenditures were discounted at 3%.

The author concluded that in the first five years from baseline the population of smokers aged 25 and over incurred excess medical expenditures totaling

$187 billion, or $2,324 per smoker. For the population of smokers in 1985, more than half of the $187 billion in excess expenditures in the next five years was paid by private insurance, $34 billion was paid out of pocket, $30 billion by Medicare, and $22 billion by Medicaid. On an individual basis, total lifetime medical expenditures for male moderate smokers (fewer than 25 cigarettes a day) averaged $32,891, 21% higher than the $27,276 for never smokers. For females, lifetime medical expenditures for moderate smokers amounted to $48,918 because they live longer than men, 14% higher than for never-smokers.

Viscusi (1995) study

This paper assesses the appropriate cigarette tax needed to address potential market failures. After comprehensive and detailed calculations of the financial externalities of smoking, the author concludes that on balance, smokers do not cost society resources because of their smoking, but rather save society money. Evidence presented indicated that the cost saving that result because of premature deaths of smokers through their lower Social Security and pension costs will more than compensate for the added costs imposed by smokers, chiefly through higher health insurance costs.

Barendregt *et al.* (1997) study

The researchers analyzed the health care costs from smoking-related diseases and for the treatment of non-smoking diseases of old age in the Netherlands. According to this study by Dutch researchers, health care costs for smokers at a given age were as much as 40% higher than those for nonsmokers. In a population in which no one smoked, the costs would be 7% higher among men and 4% higher among women than the costs in the current mixed population of smokers and nonsmokers. They used three life tables to examine the effect of smoking on health care costs – one for a mixed population of smokers and nonsmokers, one for the population of smokers, and one for the population of nonsmokers. They also used a dynamic model to estimate the effects of smoking cessation on health care costs over time. The researchers concluded that if people stopped smoking, there would be savings in health care costs, but only in the short term. Eventually, smoking cessation would lead to increased health care costs.

DISCUSSION

Smoking-attributable illnesses comprise a wide range of disorders and the prevalence of these disorders is high, resulting in high use of medical services and considerable costs to society in productivity losses. Table II lists the direct smoking costs of the prevalence-based national studies and compares them with the total personal health care expenditures in the United States. Estimates of the cost of smoking have been developed by various researchers during the past three decades employing different data bases and methodologies. Direct smoking costs estimates are relatively consistent in terms of their percentage of personal health care expenditures, ranging around 5 and 6 percent, except for two studies (Hedrick, 1971 and OTA, 1993) that yielded lower percentages and the most recent study (Miller *et al.*, 1998) that yielded a higher percentage.

Table II Direct smoking costs of prevalence-based studies as percent of personal health care expenditures, United States

Study	Year	Direct Smoking Costs (Billions)[1]	Personal Health Care Expenditures (Billions)[2]	% Direct of Personal Health Care Expenditures
Hedrick (1971)	1966	$ 1.1	$ 38.9	2.8%
Kristein (1977)	1975	5.2	114.5	4.5
Luce & Schweitzer (1978)	1976	8.2	130.5	6.3
Rice *et al.* (1986)	1980	14.4	217.0	6.6
Rice *et al.* (1986)	1984	23.3	341.5	6.8
PHS (1990)	1985	23.7	376.4	6.3
OTA (1985)	1985	22.0	376.4	5.8
OTA (1993)	1990	20.8	614.7	3.4
Bartlett *et al.* (1994)	1987	21.9	449.7	4.9
Bartlett *et al.* (1994)	1993	50.0	787.0	6.4
Miller *et al.* (1998b)	1993	72.7	787.0	9.2

[1] See Table I. [2] National Center for Health Statistics, 1998, Table 124, page 342.

The direct cost of smoking amounted to $72.7 billion in the Miller *et al.*, (1998) study, representing 9.2 percent of total personal health expenditures in 1993. This latter percentage is about 50 percent higher than earlier estimates. As noted earlier, the higher smoking cost estimates in this study compared with the earlier study (Bartlett *et al.*, 1994) are due to a variety of technical changes.

Differences in estimates over the years reflect several types of changes. First, the prevalence of smoking years has declined from 37.1 percent of adults in the United States (persons 25 years of age and over) in 1974 to 25.1 percent in 1995 (NCHS, 1998, Table 63). The effect of this declining trend would be to lower smoking cost estimates. However, there have been significant changes in the methods of estimating smoking-attributable fractions and expenditures over the time period studied. The earliest studies used physicians' opinions as a basis for smoking-attributable fractions. Later estimates have used smoking-attributable fractions based on survey data reporting utilization of hospital and physician services for smokers and nonsmokers. The latest estimates employed sophisticated regression modeling techniques that allowed for control of confounding variables and improved modeling of health and behavioral effects of smoking on expenditures.

Another important factor contributing to the differences found in smoking cost studies is that the data sets available have steadily changed and have generally improved. For example, the National Health Interview Survey on which several earlier smoking cost studies were based has no expenditure data. By comparison, the National Medical Expenditure Survey used in the more recent studies in combination with the state Behavioral Risk Factor Surveillance System contain information on smoking and other behavioral risk factors, utilization of health care services, and expenditures for health care for each individual surveyed. Finally, valid differences of opinion exist regarding analytical methods and approaches, as well as interpretation of findings among researchers. These differences are reflected in the results of the cost of smoking studies reviewed in this paper.

CONCLUSIONS

Two types of cost of smoking studies have been reviewed in this paper: prevalence-based and incidence-based studies. There are many cost-effectiveness studies of smoking cessation in the literature that are not covered here (AHCPR, 1998). The most recent study by Miller and his colleagues (1998) shows that one out of eleven personal health care dollars in the United States is spent on health care for people suffering from diseases caused by smoking or diseases exacerbated by smoking. In addition, considerable measurable losses in productivity are incurred by people who are ill and disabled and die prematurely from smoking-related diseases.

Strategies for tobacco control in the United States are multiple, including activities focused on prevention, treatment, and cessation, reduction of exposure to environmental tobacco smoke, counter advertising and counter promotion of tobacco products, tax incentives, and product regulation. Effective interventions must be found to prevent and ameliorate the adverse health effects of smoking and eventually reduce the cost of smoking.

REFERENCES

Agency for Health Care Policy and Research (AHCPR) (1997), *The Cost Effectiveness of AHCPR'S Smoking Cessation Guideline,* U.S. Department of Health and Human Services, Washington, DC.

Barendregt, J.J., Bonneux, L. and Van der Maas, P.J. (1997), "The Health Care Costs of Smoking", *New England Journal of Medicine,* Vol. 337, pp. 1052-1057.

Bartlett, J.C., Miller, L.S., Novotny, T., Rice, D.P. and Max, W. (1994), "Medical Expenditures Attributable to Cigarette Smoking – United States, 1993", *Morbidity Mortality Weekly Report*, Vol. 43, pp. 469-472.

Boden, L.I. (1976), "The Economic Impact of Environmental Disease on Health Care Delivery", *Journal of Occupational Medicine*, Vol. 18, pp. 467-472.

Canadian Department of National Health and Welfare (1967), *The Estimated Cost of Certain Identifiable Consequences of Cigarette Smoking Upon Health, Longevity, and Property in Canada in 1966,* Research and Statistics Directorate, Ottawa, Canada.

Centers for Disease Control (CDC) (1989), *Reducing the Health Consequences of Smoking: 25 Years of Progress: A Report of the Surgeon General*, Office on Smoking and Health, Department of Health and Human Services, DHHS Pub. No. 89-8411, Washington, DC.

Centers for Disease Control (CDC) (1992), *SAMMEC 2.1. Smoking-Attributable Mortality, Morbidity, and Economic Costs: Computer Software and Documentation*, Office on Smoking and Health, Atlanta, GA.

Cooper, B.S. and Rice, D.P. (1976), "The Economic Cost of Illness Revisited", *Social Security Bulletin*, Vol. 39, pp. 21-34.

Forbes, S.F. and Thompson, M.E. (1983), "Estimating the Health Care Costs of Smokers", *Canadian Journal of Public Health*, Vol. 74, pp. 183-190.

Freeman, R.A., Rowland, C.R, Smith, M.C., Shull, S.C. and Gardner, D.D. (1976), "Economic Cost of Pulmonary Emphysema: Implications for Policy on Smoking and Health", *Inquiry*, Vol. 13, pp. 15-22.

Hammond, E.C. (1966), "Smoking in Relation to the Death Rates of 1 Million Men and Women", in: Haenszel W. (Ed.), *Epidemiological Approaches to the Study of Cancer and Other Disease,* National Cancer

Institute Monograph No. 19, US Government Printing Office, Washington, DC., pp. 127-204.

Hedrick, J.L. (1971), "The Economic Costs of Cigarette Smoking", *HSMHA Health Reports,* Vol. 86, pp. 179-182.

Hodgson, T.A. (1992), "Cigarette Smoking and Lifetime Medical Expenditures", *Milbank Quarterly,* Vol. 70, pp. 81-125.

Hodgson, T.A. and Kopstein, A.N. (1984), "Health Care Expenditures for Major Diseases in 1980", *Health Care Financing Review,* Vol. 5, pp. 1-12.

Kristein, M.M. (1977), "Economic Issues in Prevention", *Preventive Medicine,* Vol. 6, pp. 252-64.

Leu, R.E. and Schaub, T. (1983), "Does Smoking Increase Medical Expenditures?", *Social Science and Medicine,* Vol. 17, pp. 1907-1914.

Leu, R.E. and Schaub, T. (1985), "More on the Impact of Smoking on Medical Care Expenditures", *Social Science and Medicine,* Vol. 21, pp. 825-827.

Lippiatt, B.C. (1990), "Measuring Medical Cost and Life Expectancy Impacts of Changes in Cigarette Sales", *Preventive Medicine,* Vol. 19, pp. 515-532.

Luce, B.R. and Schweitzer, S.O. (1978), "Smoking and Alcohol Abuse: A Comparison of Their Economic Consequences", *New England Journal of Medicine,* Vol. 298, pp. 569-571.

Manning, W.G., Keeler, E.B., Newhouse, J.P., Sloss, E.M. and Wasserman, J. (1989), "The Taxes of Sin: Do Smokers and Drinkers Pay Their Way?" *Journal of the American Medical Association,* Vol. 261, pp. 1604-1609.

Miller, L.S., Zhang, X., Novotny, T., Rice, D.P. and Max W. (1998a), "State Estimates of Medicaid Expenditures Attributable to Cigarette Smoking, Fiscal Year 1993", *Public Health Reports,* Vol. 113, pp. 140-51.

Miller, L.S., Zhang, X., Rice, D.P. and Max, W. (1998b), "State Estimates of Total Medical Expenditures Attributable to Cigarette Smoking, 1993", *Public Health Reports,* Vol. 113, pp. 56-98.

National Center for Health Statistics (NCHS) (1998), *Health, United States, 1998 With Socioeconomic Status and Health Chartbook,* DHHS Publication No. PHS 98-1232, Hyattsville, MD.

Newhouse, J.P. (1974), "A Design for a Health Insurance Experiment", *Inquiry,* Vol. 11, pp. 5-27.

Office of Technology Assessment (OTA) (1985), *Smoking-Related Deaths and Financial Costs,* OTA Staff Memorandum, Health Program, US Congress, Washington, DC.

Office of Technology Assessment (OTA) (1993), *Smoking-Related Deaths and Financial Costs: Office of Technology Assessment Estimate for 1990,* Statement of Herdman, R., Hewitt, M. and Laschober, M. before the Senate Special Committee on Aging, Washington, DC.

Oster, G., Colditz, G.A. and Kelly, N. L. (1984), "The Economic Costs of Smoking and Benefits of Quitting for Individual Smokers", *Preventive Medicine,* Vol. 13, pp. 377-389.

Public Health Service (PHS) (1990), "Smoking-Attributable Mortality, Years of Potential Life Lost, and Economic Costs: State Specific Estimates, 1985", in: *Smoking and Health: A National Status Report,* 2nd Edition, Centers for Disease Control, Office on Smoking and Health, DHHS Publication No. 87-8396, Rockville, MD., pp. 37-48.

Rice, D.P. (1966), *Estimating the Cost of Illness,* Health Economics Series, PHS Publication No. 6, US Government Printing Office, Washington, DC.

Rice, D.P., Hodgson, T.A. and Kopstein, A.N. (1985), "The Economic Cost of Illness: A Replication and Update", *Health Care Financing Review,* Vol. 7, pp. 61-80.

Rice, D.P., Hodgson, T.A., Sinsheimer, P., Browner, W. and Kopstein, A.N. (1986), "The Economic Costs of the Health Effects of Smoking, 1984", *Milbank Quarterly*, Vol. 64, pp. 489-547.

Rice, D.P. and Max W. (1992), *The Cost of Smoking in California, 1989,* California State Department of Health Services, Sacramento, CA.

Shultz, J.M., Novotny, T.E. and Rice, D.P. (1991), "Quantifying the Disease Impact of Cigarette Smoking with SAMMEC II Software", *Public Health Reports,* Vol. 106, pp. 326-333.

Viscusi, W.K. (1995), "Cigarette Taxation and the Social Consequences of Smoking", in: Poterba, J. (Ed.), *Tax Policy and the Economy,* National Bureau of Economic Research, MIT Press, Cambridge, MA.

2

HUMAN CAPITAL AND DEMOGRAPHIC APPROACHES TO ESTIMATING THE EXTERNAL COSTS OF SMOKING

DAVID COLLINS
HELEN LAPSLEY

INTRODUCTION

The issue of the social costs of smoking is one in which governments and public health community groups show a keen interest. Estimates of private and/or external costs of smoking have been produced for several advanced countries including Australia (Collins and Lapsley, 1996), Canada (Single *et al.,* 1996, Finland (Pekurinen, 1992), New Zealand (Easton, 1997), the United States (Schultz, Novotny and Rice, 1990) and now Switzerland. Such studies tend to be very influential in attracting both private and public support for anti-smoking policies. However, the methodologies used in such cost research studies, and the interpretation of their results, are open to considerable discussion. In spite of this fact, the public interpretation of these results tends to be largely uncritical.

The conventional method of estimating smoking externalities is the human capital approach. The present authors, in studies of the external costs of drug abuse (including tobacco) in Australia, have adopted an alternative technique which might be called the demographic approach. As a contribution to the methodological discussion, this paper considers some problems which have been identified with the human capital approach and considers the extent to which some of these might be alleviated by the demographic methodology. The paper confines itself to a consideration of issues directly related to the human capital and demographic approaches. It does not purport to be a review of cost estimation methodologies as a whole (for a survey of methodological issues see Single *et al.*, 1995).

THE HUMAN CAPITAL APPROACH

Because smoking produces a substantial reduction in life expectancy and because a significant proportion of the premature mortality is in the working age population, smoking causes present and future production losses. The human capital (HC) approach estimates, as one of the costs of tobacco use, the value of the loss of present and future production, discounted back to the year for which the costs are to be estimated. It could in principle be argued that similar capital techniques should be applied to other externalities for which smoking implies a future time stream of costs (for example, the production losses resulting from extended worker disability, and the health care costs over the remaining, sickness-affected, years of still-surviving smokers). In practice, these other costs tend to be estimated simply on an annual basis. Human capital techniques tend to be applied to the effects of mortality but not of morbidity.

We proceed to consider some of the issues related to the HC approach.

Interpretation of HC estimates

In general, cost estimate studies tend to devote little attention to interpretation of their results. This interpretation is not, in practice, totally straightforward because some of the estimates represent discounted present values of future time streams.

The results of HC estimates are usually represented as "the external costs of smoking in year X". There is more than one possible interpretation of this description. One interpretation might be "the external costs of smoking *which were borne in year X*". This will be in almost all cases inaccurate as a result of the discounting of a future time stream of costs back to its present value. A very significant proportion of the costs is incurred in periods subsequent to year X rather than in the year itself. A possible alternative interpretation might be "the external costs of smoking *which was undertaken in year X*". This also is wrong because almost all the external costs of smoking result from smoking in previous years (major exceptions being those resulting from pollution, environmental degradation, and cigarette-related fires and bushfires). Indeed many of the costs become evident only after very considerable lags, sometimes of up to thirty or forty years. The corollary of this fact is that, even if smoking prevalence were reduced to zero, smoking costs would continue to be experienced for many years.

The correct interpretation of conventional human capital-based estimates is: *the current value of the time stream of current and future external costs incurred as a result of past and present smoking*. It is difficult to convey this interpretation to non-economists. Furthermore, the policy implications of these estimates are unclear. They do not represent the costs actually incurred in any particular year, nor do they represent the potential returns available to anti-smoking policies in any given year. The HC approach has real interpretative problems.

These costs are estimated in relation to some (almost always) implicit counterfactual situation of past and present smoking prevalence rates of zero. Since it is, in practical terms, impossible to achieve zero prevalence rates the aggregate cost estimate gives no indication of the potential public benefits to be achieved by policies to reduce smoking prevalence. These potential benefits, which can be termed avoidable costs, will be much lower than the estimated aggregate costs. Research which the present authors have conducted indicate that, in Australia, avoidable costs represent about 45% of aggregate costs (as against about 85% for alcohol) (see Collins and Lapsley, 1996).

Choice of discount rate

Valuation using the HC approach is crucially dependent upon choice of the discount rate. An indication of the potential sensitivity of cost estimates to choice of the discount rate is given in Table I by SAMMEC II estimates of the present value of forgone future earnings of male victims of smoking at different ages and discount rates.

Table I Present value of future earnings, 1985

Age	Discount Rate		
	4%	6%	10%
	$	$	$
1-4	454,561	236,117	75,494
20-24	745,680	541,021	324,215
40-44	561,016	471,190	350,066

Sources: Schultz, Novotny and Rice (1990) pp. 68-69.

The difficulty is that there is no objective basis for the choice of discount rate. There is the theoretical issue of whether the choice should reflect the social opportunity cost rate or the social time preference rate, and the practical issue of quantifying either of these rates. In practice, cost estimate studies tend either to choose a particular discount rate with scant justification or, more usually, to indicate the sensitivity of the results to a range of rates. Given the sensitivity referred to above, these results can be somewhat indeterminate. Users of the research output often show a tendency to choose the discount rate yielding the result most amenable to their desired objective. This is a common problem in the broader field of project evaluation.

Some researchers studying the lifetime costs of smokers and nonsmokers have suggested that the use of discounting in this exercise is inappropriate, that is that the correct rate is 0% (see Barendregt, Bonneux and van der Maas, 1997). However, if these research results are to be used to inform the development of public policies towards smoking, discounting should be an integral part of the analysis.

Where benefit/cost analysis or policy/programme evaluation is involved the HC approach is indispensable and so the choice of a discount rate is unavoidable. However, estimation of the aggregate external costs of smoking is not benefit/cost analysis and, thus, alternative estimation methodologies may be appropriate.

Net versus gross costs of smokers

Debate about appropriate public policy towards smoking pays great attention to the public and private medical expenditure costs attributable to smoking. Epidemiological evidence clearly indicates that significant proportions of health care budgets are involved in treating smoking-attributable diseases (English, Holman *et al.*, 1995) and that smoking reduces life expectancy (U.S. Department of Health and Human Services, 1989). Thus smoking leads to some health expenditure reduction as a result of avoidance of the need to expend health resources on people who, had they not smoked, would still be alive. Smoking-attributable diseases are, on average, more expensive to treat than other diseases but nonsmokers live longer and so place demands on health care systems over longer periods of time. Estimation of the lifetime health cost differential is complicated by the effects of environmental tobacco smoke, which means that the health care costs of nonsmokers are partially attributable to smokers.

Smoking-attributable *net* health care costs (taking into account the impact of premature mortality) are certainly less than *gross* costs. It is clear that, when studying the impact of smoking on health care costs, the relevant cost measure is *net* costs. What is not clear is whether or not these net costs are positive, that is whether, over their whole lifetimes, smokers consume more health resources than nonsmokers. A substantial literature has arisen on this issue (see, for example, Leu and Schaub, 1983 and 1985, Manning *et al.*, 1989, Lippiatt, 1990, Hodgson, 1992, Barendregt, Bonneux and van der Maas, 1997).

A second, but at least equally important, issue is whether, *in any particular period of time*, smoking-attributable health expenditures in aggregate are at least matched by the health expenditure savings resulting from the premature deaths of smokers. Does smoking result in increased aggregate health expenditures for the community as a whole in any given year?

There is no necessary inconsistency between the existence of similar lifetime health expenditures, on the one hand, and positive net smoking-attributable health expenditures at a particular point in time, on the other. Even if lifetime expenditures were similar, the different time profiles of health expenditures on smokers and nonsmokers would mean that smoking-attributable health expenditures occurred on average at much lower ages than expenditures attributable to nonsmokers. With steady-state or even declining smoking prevalence, net smoking-attributable health expenditures could be positive for considerable periods of time. With rising smoking prevalence net health expenditures would be very substantially positive for decades.

A very interesting illustration of this point is provided by Barendregt, Bonneux and van der Maas (1997) who examine the impact of health costs in the Netherlands of complete smoking cessation. Table II summarises their results by showing the number of years, according to choice of discount rate, which would elapse before the higher longer term health care costs resulting from greater life expectancy match the lower shorter term costs resulting from lower smoking-related morbidity.

Table II Number of elapsed years before health cost break-even resulting from complete smoking cessation, Netherlands

Discount rate	Number of elapsed years
0%	26
3%	31
5%	37
10%	>50

In order to move from estimates of the net lifetime health care costs of smokers to net annual smoking-attributable health care costs, demographic analysis is required. Comparison must be made between population structures currently existing as a result of actual smoking experience and those which would have existed in a theoretical counterfactual situation of zero past or present smoking prevalence. Without demographic analysis it is not possible to produce estimates of net annual health care costs.

Similar analysis can be applied to the impact of smoking on public income maintenance expenditures such as sickness benefits and age pensions. Smoking may cause an increase in expenditures on sickness benefit payments, as a result of higher morbidity, but reductions in age pension expenditures, as a result of premature mortality. Analysis of the budgetary impact of smoking should take account of these effects and so requires demographic analysis. It should be noted that, to a large extent, these types of expenditures are transfer payments rather than real resource costs.

Most aggregate cost studies estimate gross, rather than net, smoking-attributable costs even though the net cost measure give a more accurate impact of smoking on total external costs. It should be stressed that the costs referred to here are tangible costs only. Cost estimation must also pay due attention to intangible costs such as pain, suffering and loss of life. If this is not done we might be tempted into the conclusion that the community could reap net benefits from the premature deaths of smokers, as a result of savings in health care and other expenditures.

Macroeconomic impacts of smoking

Another problem relates to the general equilibrium impacts of smoking or of reduced smoking prevalence. It is often argued that if the tobacco industry ceased to exist, or contracted substantially, as a result of public anti-smoking policies, there would be substantial loss of employment, output and income. These potential losses are represented as community benefits of smoking. The difficulty with this analysis arises from the implicit assumptions that the opportunity cost of resources used in the production of tobacco is zero and that expenditure on tobacco would not be largely or fully replaced by expenditures on other goods or services. Both these assumptions appear impossible to justify. If such a logic were pursued there would be no benefit from microeconomic reform in general, since all resources released as a result of that process would have no alternative uses. It is difficult to imagine that agricultural resources used in the production of tobacco would have zero opportunity cost and it is impossible to imagine that manufacturing and distributive resources employed in the tobacco industry would have no alternative use. However, even if these unlikely hypotheses turned out to be accurate, there would still be compensatory stimulatory effects resulting from higher levels of saving and, consequently, from lower interest rates. Industry estimates of the macroeconomic impacts of declines in smoking prevalence tend to be highly overstated (for evidence on this point see Warner and Fulton, 1994, Buck *et al.*, 1995).

A similar problem arises in valuing production losses resulting from smoking. If there were high levels of unemployment the loss of production might be small or zero (because the sick or prematurely deceased could presumably be replaced by workers who otherwise would be unemployed). The costs of smoking borne by society would apparently be much lower in periods of high unemployment than in periods of low unemployment. Increases in unemployment would apparently reduce external smoking costs. Thus the HC approach should require prediction of future unemployment rates and of the extent to which skills lost to the work force as a result of tobacco-attributable morbidity and mortality are available in the unemployed work force. Such predictions over the extended periods of time involved in the HC approach are problematic, to say the least.

In practice, smoking involves production losses even when it does not result in sickness severe enough to remove the worker from the workplace, either temporarily or permanently. These costs, which result from both active and passive smoking, can be reduced productivity resulting from non-chronic disease (for example, respiratory diseases, coughs, effects of carbon monoxide, eye irritation) plus the costs resulting from smoking rituals, litter clean-up and the cleansing of dirty air (Kristein, 1989). It is difficult to accept that the labour market works so efficiently as to internalise these smoking costs on the smoker. It is, in the case of passive smoking, impossible to believe.

DEMOGRAPHIC COST ESTIMATES

The present authors, with the assistance of a demographer, have applied the demographic approach to an estimation of the external costs of tobacco, alcohol and illicit drugs in Australia (Collins and Lapsley, 1996). This methodology has been applied at various times in relation to net health care costs and budgetary cost but had not, to our knowledge, previously been applied to estimation of the aggregate costs attributable to a particular drug. It has subsequently been applied to produce aggregate estimates in New Zealand (Easton, 1997).

The demographic approach compares the population size and structure (by age group and sex) as they exist in the year of analysis with a hypothetical alternative population calculated on the basis of assumed zero rates of prevalence over a relevant period. In the Australian study it was assumed that 40 years would be a period of time sufficient to have eliminated all the demographic effects of smoking.

Table III below illustrates the results of such a calculation for Australia in 1992. Column 2 gives the male population. Column 3 gives the number of additional males who would have been alive had there been no prior smoking. Column 4 expresses Column 3 as a percentage of Column 2. Columns 5-7 give the same information for females.

Table III The impact of smoking upon population size and structure, Australia, 1992

Age	Male Population	Increase No Tobacco	Percentage Increase	Female Population	Increase No Tobacco	Percentage Increase
(1)	(2)	(3)	(4)	(5)	(6)	(7)
0	656002	529	0.08%	623262	381	0.06%
5	655526	720	0.11%	622554	520	0.08%
10	642479	782	0.12%	607992	570	0.09%
15	679344	1029	0.15%	645253	754	0.12%
20	725997	1262	0.17%	705969	943	0.13%
25	692022	1496	0.22%	688218	1149	0.17%
30	725155	1730	0.24%	724409	1331	0.18%
35	673398	2036	0.30%	675412	1517	0.22%
40	654344	2538	0.39%	642470	1659	0.26%
45	561497	2646	0.47%	538532	1213	0.23%
50	447012	4301	0.96%	424484	1489	0.35%
55	373480	8144	2.18%	365469	2619	0.72%
60	361865	16837	4.65%	364893	5119	1.40%
65	325109	27771	8.54%	352757	8654	2.45%
70	239133	33212	13.89%	292853	11469	3.92%
75	162352	35500	21.87%	229403	14045	6.12%
80	88423	28985	32.78%	151535	12898	8.51%
85	47821	25754	53.86%	116169	14090	12.13%
Total	8710959	195272	2.24%	8771634	80420	0.92%

Source: Collins and Lapsley (1996). The demographic calculations were carried out by Professor John Pollard, Professor of Actuarial Studies, Macquarie University, Sydney.

This analysis permits comparison of the costs in the actual situation and the hypothetical zero prevalence counterfactual situation. The difference between the two can be viewed as the net tangible cost of smoking. This net cost concept can be defined quite specifically as: *the value of the net resources which in a given year are unavailable to the community for consumption or investment purposes as a result of past or present smoking.* To these costs must be added intangible costs such as pain, suffering and loss of life which, when reduced, do not release resources for other uses.

The demographic approach, allied to this definition of cost, has certain advantages:

- It estimates the costs which are actually incurred in a given year rather than the present value of the future costs incurred as a result of current mortality. This concept accords much more closely with the normal interpretation of these estimates and can be used as a basis for estimating the annual benefits available to tobacco control policies.

- It does not require use of a discount rate and so avoids the problems inherent in that choice.

- It implies no judgement about the uses to which the released resources would be put. No judgement is necessary about future unemployment rates or reactive government policies, for example macroeconomic policies.

- It permits clarification of certain issues relating to the resources' "benefits" accruing from smoking-attributable premature mortality. These include the net health care costs of smoking, consumption resources saved as a result of the mortality of both active and passive smokers and the net budgetary impact of smoking.

In its turn the demographic approach throws up some methodological problems not encountered with the HC approach. These relate to an estimation of the size and structure of the hypothetical alternative population. They include:

- Determination of the period for which the counterfactual assumption of zero smoking prevalence is to be made. The problem here is the fact that the longer the period is, the less relevant will be the current smoking etiological (that is, attributable) fractions and the less accurate and useful are likely to be the mortality and morbidity data. Applying the attributable fractions applicable to a particular year to death statistics for earlier years can be problematical since smoking prevalence may well have changed and other factors are likely to have had major impacts on deaths from various causes (for example, changes in lifestyle and medical technology).

- Accounting for, and quantifying, the demographic results of the full range of smoking-attributable mortality. Some studies of smokers' lifetime health care costs have used unduly narrow ranges of attributable causes of death (see, for example, Leu and Schaub, 1983 and 1985). The

Australian study benefited greatly from having access to the comprehensive epidemiological evidence (except in relation to passive smoking) of English, Holman *et al.* (1995).

- Accounting for second order effects such as the births which might have occurred had the persons who died from smoking-related causes lived longer, and even the children of these resulting children. In the case of smoking these effects are likely to be relatively small since the major component of smoking-related mortality occurs at ages beyond the normal child bearing years. This would be less true if the effects of mortality attributable to alcohol or illicit drugs were being studied.

- Accounting for policy responses to smoking-attributable mortality, for example the adjustment of immigration quotas to compensate for worker mortality.

SPECIFIC ISSUES OF THE DEMOGRAPHIC APPROACH

Health care costs

The demographic approach permits estimation of the net health care resources used in a particular year which are attributable to smoking. The health care experience of the actual population is compared with the estimated health care expenditures which would have been incurred on behalf of the hypothetical alternative, of the non-smoking population. This analysis takes into account the actual smoker average annual health care costs compared with the average costs attributable to nonsmokers. The Collins and Lapsley (1996) analysis was unable to estimate the impact of environmental tobacco smoke on the health care costs of nonsmokers. Thus, the health care savings attributable to smoking have almost certainly been overstated. The appearance recently of more comprehensive epidemiological information on passive smoking (see, for example, California Environment Protection Agency, 1997) should make it possible to correct for this overstatement.

Production costs and consumption benefits

Comparison of the actual and hypothetical populations, in terms of both sex and age structure, yields estimates of differences in the working age population, from which can be derived estimates of work force size.

Application of appropriate data on workplace productivity yields estimates of the potential loss of paid production resulting from smoking. The tangible cost definition proposed here – the resources which would have been available for consumption or investment purposes – removes the need to consider whether the hypothetical alternative work force would have been experiencing higher unemployment rates than the actual work force.

Aggregate cost estimates should also incorporate estimates of the value of the loss of unpaid production, for example household services and charitable work. These estimates can be derived from comparison of the two alternative non-workforce populations.

The shorter life expectancy of smokers, which translates into a lower total population, will reduce the call on the community's consumption resources. These reduced resources should logically be set against the production losses attributable to smoking. There are, at the same time, countervailing intangible costs in that, had they still been alive, the prematurely dead would have been enjoying consumption, the value of which would, at the very least, have matched the market value of these goods and services.

In the Australian study (Collins and Lapsley, 1996) the tangible consumption benefits are shown to substantially exceed total paid production costs but, in their turn, are substantially outweighed by the unpaid production losses. This effect arises because tobacco-attributable mortality tends to occur late in the working life or after retirement age. The effect is much less pronounced in relation to alcohol-attributable mortality, mainly as a result of road accident deaths.

Budgetary impacts of smoking

Studies of the impact of smoking on public sector expenditures and revenues tend to concentrate on smoking-attributable expenditures, on the one hand, and tobacco tax revenues, on the other. While smoking generates tobacco tax revenue, it can be expected, at the same time, to reduce revenue from other taxes. For example, the paid production loss resulting from the smaller working population will result in reduced revenue from taxes on personal income and payrolls. The reduced consumption expenditures of a smaller population will lead to reduced revenue from taxes on consumption and imports. These revenue reductions should be set against the revenue yielded by tobacco taxes.

Budgetary analyses of smoking often overstates relevant tobacco tax revenue because they incorporate the *total* revenue from indirect taxes on tobacco. This implies that the tobacco industry would, in the absence of taxes which specifically target the industry, be required to pay no other indirect taxes at all. It is incorrect to attribute all tobacco tax revenue being raised to compensate the community for smoking-related externalities, rather than attributing some of the revenue to the tax burden which is inevitable borne by all industries, whether or not they impose negative externalities.

Comparison of actual and hypothetical populations permits the estimation of the alternative levels of income and expenditure, and so the tax revenue loss attributable to smoking.

Valuing loss of life

Aggregate cost estimates attempt to place a value on the loss of life attributable to smoking. The cost definition implicit in demographic studies of annual costs requires valuation of loss of a year's living rather than loss of a life. Life valuation techniques will be just as readily applicable to either concept.

THE SOCIAL COSTS OF TOBACCO IN AUSTRALIA: AN ILLUSTRATION OF THE USE OF THE DEMOGRAPHIC APPROACH

The Collins and Lapsley (1996) Australian study of the social costs of tobacco has a number of features which differentiate the findings from those of other tobacco cost studies. The cost estimates are presented for the separate years 1988 and 1992. The 1988 study, which was completed in 1991, reflects the data which were available to the researchers at that time. The 1992 study, which was published in 1996, drew on a much more comprehensive data set. The additional and more comprehensive data available to the second study, and the resultant calculations, showed that the costs of smoking in Australia had increased from SFm 9,173.8 in 1988 to SFm 10,753.4 in 1992 at constant prices, – an increase in real costs of 17.2%. Detailed analysis of health care costs for this study resulted in the identification of total health care costs resulting from tobacco abuse, together with estimation of the savings resulting from premature deaths. This calculation showed that savings from premature deaths represented 48% of gross total health costs in 1992.

While both studies identified a number of costs which are real but cannot yet be quantified, including most notably the costs associated with passive smoking, nevertheless the Australian data which were available for the 1992 study are of particular significance. Most importantly, the calculation of etiological fractions which was undertaken by English, Holman *et al.* (1995) identified morbidity and mortality associated with cigarette smoking and estimated the number of hospital episodes and hospital bed days in Australia. From these fractions, it was possible to estimate the relevant episodes of hospital care attributable to smoking.

Australia is fortunate in that there are reliable national data related to the provision of health care services, to which the tobacco-related etiological fractions can be applied. Hospital data with admissions by diagnostic category, bed days and lengths of stay are collected for both public and private sector hospitals. Between the first and second cost study, case-mix costing data for Australia became available, so that costs of tobacco-related hospital days were able to be accurately identified. The average cost of hospital bed days used in the first study proved to underestimate the actual costs.

Australia has a national database which records fee-for-service payments for medical services provided outside hospitals as, under the Medicare national health insurance legislation, the Commonwealth government is the only insurer for these services. The provision of extensive government subsidy for prescribed pharmaceuticals with a patient co-payment, for outside hospital health services, has resulted in a national data-base recording cost and quantity of prescribed pharmaceuticals. An Australian Bureau of Statistics (1994) study provided calculations of the value of unpaid work, so that it was possible using an individual fraction replacement cost to value the loss of non-market work due to smoking.

Table IV below, which presents results from the 1988 and 1992 studies, shows that, even without the inclusion of passive smoking data, the net health care costs attributable to smoking were positive. While governments through taxation may cover health care costs, there will still be other significant social costs which are certainly not covered.

Table IV Health care costs and savings resulting from tobacco abuse (at current prices, swiss francs)

	1988	**1988**	**1998**	**1992**	**1992**	**1992**
	Costs	**Saving from premature deaths**	**Net costs**	**Costs**	**Saving from premature deaths**	**Net costs**
	SFm	SFm	SFm	SFm	SFm	SFm
Medical	107.7	11.9	95.8	176.0	19.0	157.0
Hospital	279.3	33.1	246.2	358.5	43.5	315.0
Nursing homes	470.4	356.7	113.7	968.9	657.3	311.6
Total	857.4	401.7	455.7	1503.3	719.8	783.6

CONCLUSION

Demographic and HC studies value the loss of production resulting from tobacco-related deaths in different ways. Both compare (explicitly or implicitly) production costs in the actual situation with those which would have existed in an alternative hypothetical situation of no smoking-related deaths. The HC approach calculates the present and future production costs of deaths which occur in the current year. These studies attempt to answer the question "What are the short and long term external costs which smoking-related deaths, sickness and other effects occurring in a given year impose upon the community?" The demographic approach calculates the present production costs of deaths which have occurred in past or present years. This type of study asks "What are the external costs which past and present smoking imposes upon the community in the current year?"

The choice of approach depends upon the type of information needed. The two methodologies are complementary rather than competitive. The HC approach is necessary for benefit/cost analysis, program and policy analysis and cost effectiveness analysis, where comparison of input and output streams over time necessitates the use of discounting.

However, estimation of the aggregate external costs of smoking is not benefit/cost analysis and the major objective of these aggregate cost studies is not evaluation of some proposed program or policy but indication of the economic dimension of the smoking problem. The question which public policymakers and many members of the community think they are asking is more likely to relate to the costs borne in a particular year than to the cost borne over the future as a results of deaths, sickness etc. occurring in that year.

An important use to which these studies have been recently put in the United States is to provide the basis for quantification of damages in lawsuits against tobacco companies on the basis that tobacco consumption has imposed costs on state budgets. Estimates of the smoking-attributable expenditures should take account of any expenditure-reducing effects of premature mortality, a process which requires demographic analysis. This analysis can, in fact, shed light on several aspects of smoking-attributable costs, health care costs, the effect upon the availability of consumption and investment resources, and budgetary impacts of smoking.

The two approaches have very considerable common data requirements. The differences in data requirements relate to the use of a discount rate, on the one hand, and of past demographic and epidemiological data, on the other.

The two methodologies illustrate different aspects of the external costs which smoking imposes on the community. The development of the literature on smoking-attributable costs into two strands illustrates the need for both approaches.

REFERENCES

Australian Bureau of Statistics (1994), *Unpaid Work and the Australian Economy, 1992,* Occasional Paper, reference No. 5240.0.

Barendregt, J.J., Bonneux, L. and Van der Maas, P.J. (1997), "The Health Care Costs of Smoking", *The New England Journal of Medicine,* October 9, pp. 1052-7.

Buck, D., Godfrey, C., Raw, M. and Sutton, M. (1995), *Tobacco and Jobs. The Impact of Reducing Consumption on Employment in the UK*, Society for the Study of Addiction, Centre for Health Economics, University of York.

California Environment Protection Agency (1997), *Health Effects of Exposure to Environmental Tobacco Smoke,* Final Report, Office of Environmental Health Hazard Assessment.

Collins, D.J. and Lapsley, H.M. (1996), *The Social Costs of Drug Abuse in Australia in 1988 and 1992*, National Drug Strategy Monograph Series No. 30, Commonwealth Department of Human Services and Health, Australia.

Easton, B. (1997), *The Social Costs of Tobacco Use and Alcohol Misuse,* Public Health Monograph No. 2, Wellington School of Medicine, New Zealand.

English, D.R., Holman C.D.J. *et al.* (1995), *The Quantification of Drug Caused Morbidity and Mortality in Australia,* Commonwealth Department of Human Services and Health, Australia.

Hodgson, T.A. (1992), "Cigarette Smoking and Lifetime Medical Expenditures", *The Milbank Quarterly*, Vol. 70, No. 1, pp. 81-125.

Kristein, M.M. (1989), "Economic Issues Relating to Smoking in the Workplace", *New York State Journal of Medicine*, January.

Leu, R.E. and Schaub, T. (1983), "Does Smoking Increase Medical Care Expenditure?", *Social Science and Medicine*, Vol. 17, No. 23, pp. 1907-1914.

Leu, R.E. and Schaub, T. (1985), "More on the Impact of Smoking on Medical Expenditures", *Social Science and Medicine*, Vol. 21, No. 7, pp. 825-827.

Lippiatt, B.C. (1990), "Measuring Medical Cost and Life Expectancy Impacts of Changes in Cigarette Sales", *Preventive Medicine*, Vol. 19, No. 5, pp. 515-532.

Manning, W.G. *et al.* (1989), "The Taxes of Sin: Do Smokers and Drinkers Pay their Way?", *Journal of the American Medical Association*, Vol. 261, No. 11, pp. 1604-1609.

Pekurinen, M. (1992), *Economic Aspects of Smoking: Is There a Case for Government Intervention in Finland?,* National Agency for Welfare and Health (Finland), Research Report No. 16/1991.

Schultz, J.M., Novotny, T.E., and Rice, D.P. (1990), *SAMMEC II, Smoking-Attributable Mortality, Morbidity and Economic Costs*, US Department of Health and Human Services, October.

Single, E., Collins, D., Easton, B., Harwood, H., Lapsley, H. and Maynard, A. (1995), *International Guidelines for Estimating the Costs of Substance Abuse*, Canadian Centre on Substance Abuse.

Single, E. *et al.* (1996), *The Costs of Substance Abuse in Canada*, Canadian Centre on Substance Abuse.

U.S. Department of Health and Human Services (1989), *Reducing the Health Consequences of Smoking: 25 Years of Progress. A Report of the Surgeon General*, DHHS publication No. (CDC) 90-8416.

Warner, K.E. and Fulton, G.A. (1994), "The Economic Implications of Tobacco Product Sales in a Non-Tobacco State", *Journal of the American Medical Association,* No. 271.

3

ESTIMATING THE INDIRECT COSTS OF SMOKING USING THE FRICTION COST METHOD

MARC A. KOOPMANSCHAP

INTRODUCTION

In estimating the burden and costs of smoking for society, the non health care costs of smoking for society should not be omitted. In this paper, the indirect non health care costs of smoking (the "productivity costs") are estimated for the Netherlands.

Because there is no consensus on how to estimate productivity costs in a reliable way, this paper provides an overview of the methodological and practical issues with respect to the calculation of this type of costs. In addition the productivity costs of smoking for the Netherlands will be calculated using both the traditional human capital approach and the more recently advocated friction cost method.

DEBATE ON INDIRECT COSTS

Defining indirect costs or "productivity costs"

Because the term indirect costs may also refer to business economics indicating the costs of supporting departments in making products, we prefer the term productivity costs as recently proposed by the Washington panel (Gold *et al*, 1996).

In this paper the following definition of productivity costs is used:

Costs due to production lost and/or replacement as a result of disease, absence from work, disability or mortality of productive persons, engaged in paid or unpaid work.

According to this definition, the impact of being ill on the sick individual's income is not of primary importance, what matters is the change in production and/or the costs to replace sick workers in order to maintain production at the initial level. Income and production losses should never be added in estimating productivity costs, as this would induce double counting. Furthermore, social security benefits may not be used as a proxy for productivity costs since these benefits only represent a redistribution of wealth, not a change in wealth.

Unpaid work is included in our definition, since unpaid work is an indispensable input for the reproduction of society's wealth and therefore should not be overlooked. The productivity loss that may occur when sick persons are still at work, being less productive than usually. is also included.

With respect to mortality, this definition only refers to the economic implications of workers dying, it does *not include the value of life as such.* The latter value may be an element in cost benefit analysis. The definition of productivity costs as stated here is to be used in cost-effectiveness and cost-utility analyses, in which life as such is valued as an element of health: in natural units (lives and life-years gained) or in QALYs or DALYs, correcting for the quality of life. 'Intangible costs' of pain, suffering, discomfort etc., aspects of illness that are sometimes labelled as costs are excluded here. These consequences of disease should preferably be measured as health effects, using quality of life instruments.

The influence of illness on leisure time is not included in our definition of productivity costs, but this topic will be discussed in section three.

Inclusion of productivity costs

Equity

Inclusion of productivity costs in economic evaluation may favour health care programmes aimed at working people as compared to people without a paid job: an equal reduction of illness may save more productivity costs for (better salaried) working people. This result may conflict with equity considerations. This situation could be avoided by excluding productivity costs from economic evaluations. However, this would deny that production losses do influence the scarcity of resources and hence decrease the wealth of society. To give a full picture of productivity costs one should also value lost production related to unpaid work, diminishing adverse equity consequences. Furthermore, it would be advisable to report on possible equity implications of including productivity costs. It is the responsibility of decision makers to decide on the relative weight that they want to attach to the equity considerations, separate from the relative efficiency of interventions.

Opportunity costs versus QALYs

Recently, Gerard and Mooney argued that including non health care costs in cost-utility analysis is wrong (Gerard and Mooney, 1993). According to them, the opportunity costs of health care resources are defined only in terms of the QALYs forgone. Hence, cost utility analysis would be about generating QALYs and QALYs foregone by opportunities sacrificed. This would preclude considering productivity costs, which could only be considered in cost-benefit analysis. These authors interpret opportunity costs in a rather narrow sense. Clearly, when program A requires a similar health care budget as program B, but uses less resources than program B from a societal perspective, the additional resources becoming available when applying program A as compared to B, could be added to the health care budget (or added to budgets for education, housing and working conditions, which may contribute to health status), and could produce QALYs. Therefore, the opportunity costs in terms of QALYs foregone of program B would be larger than those of program A. So, using a societal perspective, there is no specific requirement to use cost-benefit analysis, with its valuation problems, when considering productivity costs in an economic evaluation.

Guidelines

Canadian guidelines for economic appraisal in support of reimbursement decisions regarding pharmaceuticals do not object to including productivity costs in economic evaluation studies (CCOHTA, 1994). The most recent version of the Australian guidelines suggests that economic appraisals of pharmaceuticals should present results both with and without productivity benefits and costs included, but stresses that valuation of work time gained or lost should be made explicit (Henry, 1992).

Because French, German and British guidelines and the 'Washington Panel' (Gold *et al.,* 1996) are in favour of including productivity costs in economic evaluation of health care, overall consensus seems to be growing.

Measurement of productivity costs

Most studies estimating productivity costs use the human capital approach. This method estimates the value of potentially lost production (measured as the potentially lost income) as a consequence of disease. In case of absence from paid work, labour income during the period of absence is used as an estimate for productivity costs. With respect to disability, labour income during the entire period of disability is used for estimating productivity costs. If for example a 35-year old person becomes permanently disabled, the total income foregone from age 35 onwards until the age of retirement is estimated as productivity costs. For mortality before the age of retirement, the estimation procedure is analogous.

Many authors have criticised the human capital approach. They state that the human capital method estimates the value of potential production lost, whereas the actual loss for society may be much smaller. Drummond (1992) commented in this respect: "for short term absences, a given person's work may be covered by others or made up by the sick person on his return to work. For long term absences, an individual's work can be covered by someone drawn from the ranks of the unemployed. Therefore, while absence from work may cost the individual, or that person's employer, it may not cost society very much". Thus the human capital method may overestimate the economic consequences of disease in various circumstances.

An alternative measurement method (the 'friction cost method') has been proposed to quantify productivity costs (Koopmanschap *et al.,* 1995). The basic idea is that the amount of production lost due to disease depends on the time-span organisations need to restore the initial production level. If unemployment is beyond the level of frictional unemployment, sick employees can be replaced after a necessary period of adaptation. Production losses are assumed to be confined to the period needed to replace a sick worker: the friction period. Application of the friction cost method requires information on the *frequency and length of friction periods* and the *value of productivity lost.* In order to estimate the total number of friction periods one needs data on the frequency and length of absence spells and on the incidence of disability and mortality. The length of the friction period can be based on the average vacancy duration. The friction cost method assumes that the production level is restored after (a part of) the friction period. The actual productivity costs of disease consist of the value of production lost and/or the extra costs to maintain production and, if an employee is to be replaced permanently, the costs of filling a vacancy and training new personnel. The friction cost method also takes into account several medium term macro-economic effects of absence from work and disability. For more detailed information see Koopmanschap and Rutten (1996).

The friction cost method is still a broad instrument for estimating productivity costs (as is the human capital approach) and it needs more refinement in measuring the exact consequences of short term absence from work for production and costs. The debate on the friction cost method goes on, see Johannesson and Karlsson (1997) and Koopmanschap *et al.* (1997).

RESULTS FOR THE NETHERLANDS IN 1994

To estimate the productivity costs of smoking for the Netherlands, we combined the following data:

- Costs of absence from paid work, incidence of disability and mortality by disease for the Netherlands in 1994, as estimated by both the friction cost method and the human capital method. The Netherlands disposed of nation-wide statistics on frequency and duration of absence from work by disease, age and sex, covering 58% of the workforce (CTSV, 1996). For incidence of disability the registration covers all cases by disease age and sex (GAK, 1996). Mortality data by disease, age (15-19, 20-34, 35-49, 50-64) and sex are published by the CBS (1996).

- The estimated prevalence of smoking by age and sex (Barendregt *et al.*, 1997) (see Table I).

- The rate ratios for smokers versus nonsmokers for the following diseases: ischaemic heart disease (IHD), stroke, lung cancer and COPD.

Table I Prevalence of smoking in % for the Netherlands (average for 1988-1992)

Age	Male	Female
15-19	20	20
20-34	39	37
35-49	42	36
50-64	39	27

Source: Barendregt *et al.*, 1997.

Combining prevalence and rate ratios gave for smokers the etiological fractions of morbidity per disease, by age and sex. These etiological fractions were consequently used as cost fractions, assuming that if smokers represent x% of the burden of a specific disease, they also cause x% of the productivity costs related to this disease.

Table II Rate ratio's per disease for smokers and nonsmokers

Disease	ICD-code	Rate ratio
IHD	410-414	3
Stroke	430-438	2
Lung cancer	162	10
COPD	490-496	25

Source: Barendregt *et al.*, 1997.

Table III Costs of absence from work due to smoking for the Netherlands in 1994 in million DFL (% of Net National Income)

Disease	Friction cost method	Human capital method
IHD	133	377
Stroke	20	60
Lung cancer	16	46
COPD	100	202
Total smoking	270	685
	(0.05%)	(0.12%)

% costs for men: about 85%.

According to the friction cost method (Koopmanschap and Rutten, 1996), using an average friction period of 3.2 months, total costs of absence from work were DFL 270 million, that is 0.05% of national income in 1994. Most costs are caused by ischaemic heart diseases and COPD. Using the human capital approach, the same disease pattern exists, but total costs are more than double: DFL 685 million (0.12% of NNI). This difference is due to the fact that the human capital theory counts all days absence from work (maximally 365 days per calendar year) as productivity costs, whereas the friction cost method uses a cut off point of 3.2 months.

Table IV Disability and mortality costs of smoking, according to the human capital method. Netherlands 1994 in million DFL (% of Net National Income)

Disease	Disability costs	Mortality costs
IHD	1536	1092
Stroke	342	572
Lung cancer	71	578
COPD	1401	447
Total smoking	3349	2690
	(0.6%)	(0.5%)

Table V Productivity costs of smoking versus all diseases. Netherlands 1994

Method and cost component	Smoking costs as % of all diseases
Friction costs	1.1%
Human capital	
• Absence from work	1.8%
• Disability	5.3%
• Mortality	25.6%
• Human capital total costs	6.0%

Smoking is responsible for only modest fractions of costs related to absence and disability, because smoking does not affect the major causes of absence and disability in the Netherlands: mental disorders and musculoskeletal diseases.

For mortality, the costs according to the human capital approach are substantial, since smoking affects the two major causes of death: cancer and cardiovascular diseases.

DISCUSSION

The usefulness of cost-of-illness estimates is not undisputed. Shiell, Gerard and Donaldson (1987) stated that the cost-of-illness studies cannot serve as a component in evaluating alternative demands on scarce health care resources because the cost estimates don't provide any information on the effectiveness of the related health care investments. They stated that cost of illness studies merely satisfy the curiosity on the aggregate burden of disease and that the cost estimates only quantify the benefits of the unattainable: the savings if a disease could be eradicated. Moreover they hold the opinion that the cost-of-illness results may lead to priority for programmes directed to diseases which are already costly. If past resource allocation has not been cost-effective, subsequent policy decisions would only amplify irrational spending.

Hodgson (1989) responded to this critique by stating that COI is not policy making, but may be policy relevant, by educating, informing and enlightening policy makers. He further claimed that COI should be a prominent component in cost effectiveness analyses. The latter studies also deliver evidence on effectiveness of care and hence are directly policy-relevant.

The productivity costs of smoking as estimated above only calculated the costs of smoking due to four specific disease categories. As a consequence, the real costs attributable to smoking may be somewhat underestimated, since some research indicates that smokers may also have higher rates of absence and disability related to other diseases. This may be incorporated in further research on productivity costs of smoking.

REFERENCES

Barendregt, J.J., Bonneux, L. and Van der Maas, P.J. (1997), "The Health Care Costs of Smoking", *New England Journal of Medicine,* Vol. 337, pp. 1052-1057.

CBS – Central Bureau of Statistics (1996), *Mortality Data 1994*, serie A1, Voorburg/Heerlen.

CCOHTA – Canadian Coordinating Office for Health Technology Assessment (1994), *Guidelines for Economic Evaluation of Pharmaceuticals Canada*, Ottawa, Ontario.

CTSV – College van Toezicht Sociale Verzekeringen(1996), *Absence from Work Data 1994*, Zoetermeer.

Drummond, M.F. (1992), "Cost of illness Studies: A Major Headache?", *PharmacoEconomics,* Vol. 2, No. 1.

GAK – Gemeenschappelijk AdministratieKantoor (1996), *Disability Data 1994*, Amsterdam.

Gerard, K. and Mooney, G. (1993), "QALY League Tables: Handle With Care", *Health Economics*, Vol. 2, No. 59.

Gold, M.R., Siegel, J.E., Russell, L.B. and Weinstein, M.C. (1996), *Cost-Effectiveness in Health and Medicine*, Oxford University Press, Oxford.

Henry, D.A. (1992), "The Australian Guidelines for Subsidisation of Pharmaceuticals", *PharmacoEconomics* , Vol. 2, pp. 4-22.

Hodgson, T.A. (1989), "Cost of Illness Studies: No Aid to Decision-making? Comments on the Second Opinion by Shiell *et al.*", *Health Policy,* Vol. 11, pp. 57-60.

Johannesson, M. and Karlsson, G. (1997), "The Friction Cost Method: A Comment", *Journal of Health Economics,* Vol. 16, No. 2, pp. 249-255.

Koopmanschap, M.A., Rutten, F.F.H., van Ineveld, B.M. and van Roijen, L. (1995), "The Friction Cost Method for Measuring Indirect Costs of Disease", *Journal of Health Economics,* Vol. 14, pp. 171-189.

Koopmanschap, M.A. and Rutten, F.F.H. (1996), "A Practical Guide for Calculating Indirect Costs of Disease", *PharmacoEconomics*, Vol. 10, No. 5, pp. 460-466.

Koopmanschap, M.A., Rutten, F.F.H., van Ineveld, B.M. and van Roijen, L. (1997), "Reply to Johannesson's and Karlsson's Comment", *Journal of Health Economics,* Vol. 16, No. 2, pp. 257-259.

Shiell, A., Gerard, K. and Donaldson, C. (1987), "Cost of Illness Studies: An Aid to Decision-making?" *Health Policy,* 8, pp. 317-323.

4

CONTINGENT VALUATION OR QALYs

PER-OLOV JOHANSSON

INTRODUCTION

First of all, let me comment on the title of my presentation. The title was a suggestion from the organisers, which I accepted and hence take sole responsibility for. The basic idea behind quality-adjusted life-years (QALYs) is to let the individual indicate the 'relative' *utility* he derives from a particular health profile. Typically, the utility derived from full health is set equal to unity and the utility derived from the worst possible health state (death) is set equal to zero. QALYs are often used as the benefits measure in cost-effectiveness analysis (then sometimes called cost-utility analysis) of medical treatments. Contingent valuation is a survey *method* for the estimation of the willingness-to-pay (or the willingness-to-accept-compensation) for a change in utility. In the simplest variation, respondents are asked about their maximal willingness-to-pay for a particular project. The contingent valuation method (CVM) is often used as a tool in cost-benefit analysis. I interpret the title as hinting at the question of whether we should use cost-benefit analysis or cost-utility analysis in order to assess the effects of smoking.

A LIFE-CYCLE APPROACH

In order to proceed further, we must decide what to evaluate. Let us first consider a smoker's decision problem. A smoker can possibly be assumed to look at the benefits and costs of his smoking. It is a forward-looking decision problem, where the smoker must assess the current and future benefits or the satisfaction derived from smoking; the reader is referred to the Appendix at the end of this chapter for an outline of such a model. There are costs in terms of out-of-pocket expenditures for tobacco and effects on his health and his survival probability. Possibly, he will also contribute too much or too little to public social security systems (public health care plus the pension system). The net outcome depends, among other things, on how the costs of health care and the expected length of life are affected by smoking.

Nonsmokers are also affected. Their health might be affected through passive smoking, i.e. there is an externality associated with smoking. Sometimes there are also altruistic concerns involved since nonsmokers might be concerned about the health of smokers (and vice versa). Furthermore, nonsmokers might get a share of the revenues from tobacco taxes. They are possibly also affected through public social security systems (health care, pensions, and so on) depending on whether smokers contribute too much or too little to such systems.

Even if this framework is highly simplified, it illustrates the fact that it is extremely complicated to assess the benefits and costs of smoking. The question is to know if there is a role for the contingent valuation method in such evaluations. A first and partial answer is that market prices should be able to do the job. The area to the left of the demand curve for tobacco (above the market price) yields an estimate of the consumer surplus derived from consuming tobacco.

USING MARKET DATA TO ASSESS SMOKING

In order to examine how far market prices can take us, let us leave our life cycle model outlined in the previous section, where the smoker was assumed to be forward-looking, and turn to a very simple atemporal model of a rational smoker's decision problem. Such a model is presented in the Appendix. The smoker, who is assumed to be an expected utility maximiser, derives satisfaction from his smoking. However, he also realises that smoking adversely affects his health as well as his survival probability. By examining the first-order conditions for utility maximisation, we can establish that at the optimum the marginal willingness to pay for cigarettes will be equal to the price of a cigarette. The marginal willingness to pay for cigarettes has several components. There is the monetary valuation of the satisfaction which the smoker derives from his smoking. However, conditional on being alive, smoking adversely affects health. This reduces the smoker's marginal willingness to pay. A further reduction is due to the adverse effect of smoking on the survival probability. In the model considered, the smoker consumes such a number of cigarettes that the sum of these three components is equal to the market price of a cigarette.

The value of a statistical life is often calculated in order to be able to compare the outcome of different attempts to measure the willingness to pay for risk reductions. In order to illustrate the concept, let us consider a medical treatment that saves 1 out of 1000 lives (say, by reducing the number of deaths from 6 out of a 1000 to 5 out of a 1000). Furthermore, assume that the average willingness to pay for the treatment is $4000. Then the value of a statistical life is obtained by multiplying $4000 by 1000/1. Thus, in this example the value of a statistical life is $4 million. By converting or normalising the results in this way, it is easy to compare the outcome of different valuation experiments involving different methods, different risks, and different risk reductions. It might be noted that a recent survey of the available empirical evidence finds that most of the reasonable estimates of the value of a statistical life are clustered in the $3 to $7 million range (Viscusi, 1992).

It would be an advantage if we could use the market price of cigarettes to calculate the value of a statistical life. By comparing this value with the ones obtained in the most reliable existing estimates we would be able to examine, for example, whether smokers treat risks in a rational way. However, we cannot use the market price of cigarettes to calculate the value of a statistical life. The reason is the fact that there are two unobservable utility terms in the expression (as can be seen from equation (12) in the Appendix). In addition, these unobservable terms appear with opposite signs, i.e. we don't know whether their sum is positive or negative. Thus we cannot easily use the market price to establish a lower bound or an upper bound for the value of a statistical life. It is reasonable to assume that this problem does not disappear if we turn from our simple atemporal model to a more complex life cycle utility maximisation model.

Even if we can somehow overcome these difficulties, there might be a role for the contingent valuation method. Passive smoking and altruistic concerns are not priced in the market. If we want to include such concerns in an evaluation, we must probably use survey instruments such as contingent valuation (or, for example, conjoint analysis).

THE CONTINGENT VALUATION METHOD

The contingent valuation method (CVM) is the modern name for the survey method (since the answers to a valuation question are contingent upon the particular hypothetical market described to the respondents). The method was probably first used by Davis, who used questionnaires to estimate the benefits of outdoor recreation (Davis, 1963). In their excellent book on the contingent valuation method, Mitchell and Carson list more than 100 U.S. studies based on this technique (Mitchell and Carson, 1989), while a recent survey lists 26 U.K. studies (Green *et al.*, 1990). See also the recent survey of European studies (Navrud, 1992). Since these lists were composed, a large number of new studies based on the contingent valuation technique have undoubtedly been completed. For example, one survey lists around 1400 studies related to the method (Carson *et al.,* 1993). The survey technique is thus widely used for the estimation of environmental benefits in particular, and there is a large body of knowledge on the method's advantages and disadvantages. In recent years, a number of studies using the CVM to assess health care have appeared. The reader is referred to Johansson (1995) for a brief survey of some of these studies.

Roughly speaking, the CVM collects preference information by asking individuals how much they are willing to pay for some change in the provision of a good, or what is the minimum compensation that individuals require if the change is not carried out. The most common approaches are to ask a respondent about his willingness to pay or to "mimic" a market by letting the respondent accept or reject paying a particular amount of money in exchange for the considered project/treatment. In the latter case, the bid is varied across different subsamples of the population in order to acquire information about the "demand" curve for the project/treatment.

The central problem in a contingent valuation study is to make the scenario sufficiently understandable, plausible and meaningful to respondents. The respondent must understand the characteristics of the good he is asked to value. Also, the mechanism for providing the good in a CVM must seem plausible in order to avoid scepticism that the good can or will be provided. It is both abstract and unconvincing to ask the respondent to simply *imagine* that the good (say a medical treatment or programme) will be provided.

In the case of medical treatments one also faces the problem that people have difficulties in understanding the meaning of (changes in) small risks. To illustrate, let us assume that 25 out of 10,000 forty-year old individuals will die within the next year; the estimation is based on data for the US (Johansson, 1996). A particular treatment reduces the number of deaths from 25 to 24 out of 10,000 lives. The risk of death is so small, about 0.0025, that it is difficult to understand. This is evidently also true for the treatment. On the other hand, the treatment causes quite a large relative reduction (4 percent) in the death risk. This opens up the possibility that the phrasing of the question, for example how information about risks is presented, will have a large impact on the outcome of a valuation experiment. For example, respondents might find a death risk equal to 0.0025 very different from the fact that 25 people will die, although it is 25 out of 10,000.

In addition, there is the complexity and long-run nature of the consequences of smoking. It must be extremely difficult for participants in a contingent valuation experiment to assess the relevant benefits and costs over the entire remaining life cycle. There are tricks that simplify the evaluation. For example, one might ask respondents to evaluate the consequences during the next year. Then information from respondents of different ages can be used to assess the long-run consequences (for a person of a particular age). Still, many, many complications remain.

We might also be interested in evaluations of various therapies used for giving up smoking or preventive measures taken to prevent people from starting smoking. In such evaluations there seems to be a role for survey instruments. There are either no obvious markets or if there are markets, prices are often subject to regulations. The obvious alternative is to base an evaluation on surveys. The basic problems the investigator faces are those hinted at above.

QUALITY-ADJUSTED LIFE-YEARS

Turning to QALYs, in a risky world, the approach is often used as follows (Johannesson, 1996). The individual is assumed to be an expected utility maximiser. Suppose that the individual is offered a choice between living T years with health quality h_c, possibly interpreted as his current health status, and a gamble according to which the probability is π that he will live with full health for T years and the probability is $1 - \pi$ that he will die immediately. Next, find the probability π^* that will make the individual indifferent between the two alternatives. This technique is known as the *standard gamble* technique. It follows that the probability π^* must be equal to the utility derived from current health status, i.e. $\pi^* = v(y,h_c)$, where $v(.)$ is an indirect utility function, and y denotes income. Repeating the experiment, but with current health replaced by the health status h_m achieved with a particular medical treatment, yields the utility $v(y,h_m)$ associated with the treatment. This approach can be used to calculate the present value of the number of QALYs gained from the treatment. (Thus we calculate $\Sigma_t\rho^{t-1}[v(y,hmt) - v(y,hct)]$, where $\rho \leq 1$ is a discount factor, and t refers to period t.)

Alternatively, one may use a *time trade-off* technique to estimate the utility function $v(y,h_c)$. That is, change the time horizon T so as to make the individual indifferent. This yields the time, say T^* years, with current health which the individual finds equivalent to living for T years with full health with probability π, and dying immediately with probability $1 - \pi$. Given the time horizon T^* (and the discount rate), one can directly figure out $v(y,h_c)$.

Typically, the two methods described here require in-person interviews, and the respondent is asked to provide a hypothetical answer (ultimately about his *unobservable* level of utility) to a hypothetical change in health and/or health risks. Thus the problems in using standard gambles and time trade-offs are similar to those one faces in a contingent valuation study where the respondent is asked to make a hypothetical payment in exchange for a hypothetical change in health and health risks. For a discussion of all the problems or biases one may encounter in estimating QALYs the reader is referred to Johansson (1995). There is however a difference between a CVM and the two approaches outlined here to estimate QALYs, since one can undertake experiments with real (and hence *observable*) payments in order to examine the properties of money measures of utility change. There seems to be no similar observable mechanism available in the case of QALYs.

In the future it might be possible to put a "price tag" on a QALYs, i.e. to estimate the WTP for a QALYs. Then one could "easily" go from one concept to the other. However, to the best of my knowledge this is not yet possible. Presently, the concept of QALYs seems to be most useful in analysis of the cost-effectiveness of, say, a programme aiming at preventing people from starting or continuing smoking or different medical treatments aimed at curing various diseases caused by the habit of smoking. However, as far as I can understand there are at least two fundamental methodological problems involved. Firstly, the problem is the fact that so many of the effects associated with smoking fall outside the health care system. For example, smokers pay tobacco taxes and they contribute to (typically) a pay-as-you-go pension system (see Zweifel and Breyer, 1997) on the same basis as nonsmokers. Therefore, I question the value of conventional cost-effectiveness analysis involving only the consequences that fall within the health care system. Such analyses would probably yield a biased picture of the social profitability of various anti-smoking programmes. Secondly, if the decision to become a smoker in some sense were rational, the smoker would lose QALYs by quitting. That is, he would experience a lower relative utility if he stopped smoking than if he continued to smoke. In other words, a cost-utility analysis based on, or respecting individual preferences would reject anti-smoking measures almost by definition.

CBA OR CEA/CUA?

It might seem interesting to undertake a social cost-benefit analysis (CBA) of smoking. However, from the point of view of an economist, it is the *marginal* benefits and costs that provide important information. If a project's marginal benefits exceed its marginal costs we can infer that the project is too small, and vice versa. Thus we can inform the decision-maker whether more or less resources should be devoted to the considered project. On the other hand, the *total* benefits and costs do not provide us with much information. To illustrate, even if the total benefits from car traffic exceed its costs, we can still have too much car traffic. That is, the marginal car trip can cause costs (through traffic congestion, environmental impact, and so on) that exceed the benefits of the trip. The same logic holds in the case of smoking. Thus by collecting information on the marginal social benefits and costs of smoking we should be able to infer, for example, whether tobacco is too heavily taxed or not (Choi, 1993). The idea here is that the tobacco tax should be increased so as to decrease tobacco consumption if the marginal social benefits of smoking fall short of its costs. (In the case of perfect and symmetric information, it would be possible to differentiate payments to health care and pension systems so as to reflect smoking habits. However, such information is not readily available.)

Similarly, it might be of interest to assess the marginal benefits and costs of programmes aimed at preventing people from becoming smokers or simplifying quitting the smoking habit.

I have pointed out earlier the formidable difficulties that the investigator faces in collecting information about the monetary valuation of some of the central consequences of smoking: the smoker's valuation, the monetary valuation of passive smoking and altruistic concerns, and so on. Nevertheless, I would certainly welcome attempts to undertake such evaluations. The reason is as follows. We have identified and are aware of many of the problems that investigators should expect to face. This awareness opens up the possibility of searching for and finding (new) solutions.

I do view cost-effectiveness analysis (CEA) or cost-utility analysis (CUA) and cost-benefit analysis as complementary rather than as mutually exclusive. They do provide answers to slightly different questions. A cost-benefit analysis can be used to discuss, for example, how much resources to devote to a sector, while cost-utility analysis is useful for discussion of how to allocate a fixed budget among competing alternatives. However, as mentioned earlier it seems questionable to use CEA/CUA when many of the important effects fall outside the health care system. In addition there is the problem in capturing the smoker's valuation of his smoking habit. As far as I can see, one would face similar problems in using the method to evaluate preventive programmes and programmes aimed at simplifying giving up smoking.

CONCLUDING REMARKS

This paper has been devoted to a brief discussion of the possibility of using the contingent valuation method to assess the benefits and costs of smoking. The paper also contains a brief discussion of the concept of QALYs. The conclusions of the paper might seem very pessimistic. It is obviously very difficult for respondents to assess the monetary value of small changes in (small) health risks. Similarly, the author of this paper questions the meaningfulness of QALYs in the context of a voluntary decision to take up a risky activity, for example, smoking.

Nevertheless, the contingent valuation method (or "relatives" such as conjoint analysis) could be a useful tool if properly and carefully used. However, smoking involves long-run consequences for health as well as for payments to and from social security systems. Therefore, it is important to carefully design and test the survey instrument. For example, it is probably easier for a respondent to assess a temporary, say a 1-year, change in the hazard rate than to assess a permanent change lasting over the respondent's remaining lifetime. There are techniques available for "linking" such temporary changes into permanent ones (Johannesson *et al.*, 1997). Similarly, some of the financial consequences, in particular payments to and from public pension systems, are probably easier to calculate separately rather than by asking respondents. Thus, my aim has not been to argue that the contingent valuation method cannot be used but rather to point out that the method must be used with great care and skill if one wants to assess a complicated life-cycle problem.

REFERENCES

Carson, R.T., Wright, J., Alberini, A. and Flores, N. (1993), *A Bibliography of Contingent Valuation Studies and Papers,* Natural Resource Damage Assessment, La Jolla, CA.

Choi, B.C.K. (1993), "A Cost-Benefit Analysis of Smoking in Canada", in: Huang, P.C., Lin, R.S. and Chow, L.P. (Eds.), *Health Care in the Changing Economic and Social Environment,* Research in Human Capital and Development, Vol. 7, JAI Press, London, pp. 149-75.

Davis, R.K. (1963), "Recreation Planning as an Economic Problem", *Natural Resources Journal*, Vol. 3, pp. 239-249.

Green, C.H., Tunstall, S.M., N'Jai, A. and Rogers, A. (1990), "Economic Evaluation of Environmental Goods", *Project Appraisal*, Vol. 5, pp. 70-82.

Johannesson, M. (1996), *Theory and Methods of Economic Evaluation of Health Care*, Kluwer Academic Publishers, Dordrecht.

Johannesson, M., Johansson, P.-O. and Löfgren, K.-G. (1997), "On the Value of Changes in Life Expectancy: Blips Versus Parametric Changes", *Journal of Risk and Uncertainty*, Vol. 15, pp. 221-239.

Johansson, P.-O. (1995), *Evaluating Health Risks. An Economic Approach*, Cambridge University Press, Cambridge.

Johansson, P.-O. (1996), "On the Value of Changes in Life Expectancy", *Journal of Health Economics* , Vol. 15, pp. 105-113.

Mitchell, R.C. and Carson, R.T. (1989), *Using Surveys to Value Public Goods. The Contingent Valuation Method,* Resources for the Future, Washington, D.C.

Navrud, S. (Ed.) (1992), *Valuing the Environment. The European Experience*, Oxford University Press, Oxford.

Viscusi, W. K. (1992), *Fatal Trade-offs. Public & Private Responsibilities for Risk*, Oxford University Press, New York.

Zweifel, P. and Breyer, F. (1997), *Health Economics*, Oxford University Press, Oxford.

APPENDIX

Let us consider an individual who derives satisfaction from his smoking, his consumption of other goods and services, and from his health. His instantaneous utility function is as follows:

$$u[c(t), s(t), h(t)] \tag{1}$$

where $u[.]$ is the instantaneous utility function, $c(t)$ denotes consumption at time t of goods other than tobacco, $s(t)$ denotes tobacco consumption, and $h(t)$ denotes health. In turn, health is viewed as being a negative function of his accumulated smoking over the years, $Z(t)$, and a positive function of his consumption of health goods, $H(t)$. Thus:

$$h(t) = h[Z(t), H(t)] \tag{2}$$

The accumulation of tobacco is assumed to be governed by the following equation:

$$\dot{Z}(t) = s(t) - \gamma Z(t) \tag{3}$$

where a dot refers to a time derivative and the depreciation factor γ is such that $0 \le \gamma \le 1$. If the smoker quits smoking the adverse impact of his past smoking on his health will diminish over time, at least if $\gamma > 0$.

The survivor function is as follows:

$$\mu(t) = e^{-\Delta(t)} \tag{4}$$

where $\Delta(t) = \int_0^t \delta[\tau, h(t)] d\tau$. The time derivative of $\Delta(t)$ is as follows:

$$\dot{\Delta}(t) = \delta[t, h[Z(t), H(t)]] \tag{5}$$

where $\delta[.]$ is the hazard rate, i.e. the probability that the individual will die in a short time interval $(t,t+dt)$. The hazard rate is assumed to be increasing in age, and decreasing in health. In turn, health is adversely affected by the smoker's accumulated consumption of tobacco. Even if he quits smoking today, there will be an adverse future effect on his health and, indirectly, on his survival probability.

The expected remaining present value utility at age t^c is as follows:

$$\int_{t^c}^{\infty} u[c(t), s(t), h(t)] e^{-r(t-t^c)} e^{-\Delta(t-t^c)} dt \qquad (6)$$

where r is a discount rate.

The dynamic budget constraint is assumed to be as follows:

$$\dot{k}(t) = rk(t) + (1-i)w[s(t)] + P(t) - c(t) - p(t)s(t) - p^H(t)H(t) \qquad (7)$$

where $k(t)$ denotes an asset, $rk(t)$ is capital income, i is a tax rate, on wage income, $w(t)$ denotes wage income, here as a (negative) function of smoking, $P(t)$ is a pension income, $p(t)$ is the price of tobacco, p^H is the price of health goods, and it is assumed that $w(t) > 0$ and $P(t) = 0$ for $t \leq T^p$, while $w(t) = 0$ and $P(t) > 0$ for $t > T^p$. Thus T^p denotes the time at which the individual retires.

The smoker is assumed to maximise equation (6) subject to equations (5) and (7). We will not attempt to solve the problem here. The purpose has rather been to indicate that it is quite a complex problem even though some readers might feel that the model is too simple. The model also illustrates that it is difficult to formulate a valuation question that captures all aspects of the smoker's decision problem.

Let us also consider a simple atemporal expected utility model for a smoker:

$$U = \pi(s)u[c, s, h(s)] \qquad (8)$$

where U denotes expected utility, $\pi(s)$ is the survivor probability as a (negative) function of the quantity of tobacco consumed, $u(.)$ is a utility function, conditional on being alive, c is the consumption of goods other than tobacco, and *h(s)* is his health status as a (negative) function of his smoking.

The budget constraint is as follows:

$$y = c + ps \tag{9}$$

where *y* is a fixed income, and *p* is the unit price of tobacco.

The considered smoker maximises expected utility subject to his budget constraint. Two necessary conditions for an interior solution to this maximisation problem are as follows:

$$\begin{aligned} \pi u_c &= \lambda \\ \pi_s u + \pi(u_s + u_h h_s) &= \lambda p \end{aligned} \tag{10}$$

where λ is the Lagrange multiplier associated with the budget constraint, $u_c = \partial u(.)/\partial c$, $\pi_s = \partial \pi(.)/\partial s$, $u_s = \partial u(.)/\partial s$, $u_h = \partial u(.)/\partial h$, and $h_s = \partial h(.)/\partial s$.

Combining the two first-order conditions we can define a marginal willingness to pay, *MWTP*, and a marginal cost, *MC*, for smoking:

$$\begin{aligned} &MWTP : \frac{\pi_s u + \pi(u_s + u_h h_s)}{\pi u_c} \\ &MC : p \end{aligned} \tag{11}$$

In optimum, *MWTP* = *MC*. Next, we can define the marginal value of life, *MVOL*, as follows:

$$MVOL : \frac{u}{\pi u_c} = \frac{p - (u_s + u_h h_s)/u_c}{\pi_s} \tag{12}$$

Apparently, information on the market price of tobacco, i.e. p, is not sufficient to calculate the *MVOL*. Also note that $u_s > 0$ while $u_h h_s < 0$ in equation (12).

5

WHEN DOES NON-SMOKING SAVE HEALTH CARE MONEY? THE MANY ANSWERS TO A SIMPLE QUESTION[1]

JAN J. BARENDREGT
LUC BONNEUX
PAUL J. VAN DER MAAS

INTRODUCTION

Smoking is a major health hazard, and since nonsmokers are healthier, it seems only natural that non-smoking would save health care money. Yet in the economics of health care the question arises time and again: which costs more to the health care sector, smokers who tend to die early from expensive diseases, or nonsmokers who can accumulate more health care costs because they live longer?

The Surgeon General let it be known in 1992 that "the estimated average life-time medical costs for a smoker exceed those for a nonsmoker by more than $6,000" (MacKenzie, Bartecchi and Schrier, 1994). Lippiatt estimates that 1% lower cigarette sales increases medical care costs by $405 million in the age range from 25-79 (Lippiatt, 1990). Manning *et al.* argue that although smokers incur higher medical costs, these are being balanced by tobacco taxation and a shorter life span (hence less use of pensions and

[1] The research for this paper was funded by the Dutch Ministry of Health. The results of this paper were first published by the New England Journal of Medicine (Barendregt, Bonneux and van der Maas 1997).

nursing homes) (Manning *et al.,* 1989). Leu and Schaub showed that even when looking only at health care expenditures the longer life expectancy of nonsmokers more than compensates their lower annual utilisation rates (Leu and Schaub, 1983).

The controversy is fuelled by emotions, but by methodological differences as well. Some authors only talk about medical costs, others include taxes and pensions, and yet others will even venture into the arcane realm of indirect societal costs to make their point (Elixhauser, 1990). Different methods are also employed to compare smokers' and nonsmokers' health care utilisation: some estimate costs attributable to smoking, others lifetime costs, with the deceptively simple looking life table technique often used to handle the differences in life expectancy. And, since time and money are involved, the topic of discounting future costs and savings comes up.

In this article we concentrate on the question of the health care costs of smoking by formulating six different research questions, and selecting for each the appropriate method. To simplify matters we look at medical costs only, employing data from the Netherlands. We show that while a sizeable part of health care costs can be attributed to smoking, nonsmokers nevertheless can have higher life-time costs, but that with a suitable choice of discount rate and evaluation period it would still be financially attractive when all smokers would quit. We conclude that the controversy on the health care costs of smoking is caused in part by the unavoidable arbitrariness of economic evaluation methods.

THREE DISCIPLINES

The question of smoking costs for the health care sector requires an interdisciplinary approach: methods from epidemiology, demography and economics are employed. We look at the impact of smoking on five major diseases: heart disease, stroke, lung cancer, a heterogeneous group of "other cancers", and chronic obstructive pulmonary disease (COPD). We obtained rate ratios for the 5 diseases from an overview of international literature (Van de Mheen and Gunning-Schepers, 1996). Using this rate ratio and the prevalence of smoking in a population, it is possible to calculate the proportion of the total number of cases of a disease that can be attributed to smoking, the Population Attributable Risk (PAR, or Etiologic Fraction, see appendix) (Kleinbaum, Kupper and Morgenstern, 1982).

Note that the PAR ignores the problem of competing death risks (Manton and Stallard, 1988). All people die, but without smoking they will do so (partly) from other causes, and at a higher age. To calculate at what age, we used an extension of the standard life table, the multi-state life table, that distinguishes not just between "alive" and "dead", but allows for additional states like "alive, healthy", "alive, with heart disease", etc (Schoen, 1987). With the help of the rate ratios and smoking prevalence we calculated three life tables, one describing a population with current smoking prevalences, and one each for a smokers' and a nonsmokers' population (see appendix). These three life tables form the basis of the analysis.

When future money is an issue, we enter into the economists' field of discounting. Discounting is done because of the existence of time preference: we prefer to have money (or resources) now rather than in the future (Drummond, Stoddart and Torrance, 1990). Although economists cite various reasons why time preference might exist, the phenomenon as such is not questioned. Cost-benefit analysis uses discounting to help decide which future stream of costs and benefits is preferred, with the different streams generated by alternative investment strategies. In health care this translates into the comparison of the financial consequences of different medical interventions and their follow-up. To make these streams comparable, they are converted to their Present Value, a procedure that requires choices to be made on the length of the evaluation period and the discount rate, choices with a large impact on outcome (see appendix).

Data on the epidemiology of smoking related diseases are from various studies (Bonneux *et al.,* 1994; Eindhoven Cancer Registry, 1991; Niessen *et al.,* 1993; Weel *et al.,* 1987). Mortality data, both disease specific and total, were obtained from Statistics Netherlands (CBS, Published annually). Smoking data from the Dutch Foundation of public health and smoking (Foundation of Public Health and Smoking, 1993), rate ratio's from an overview of the international literature (Table I, source (Van de Mheen and Gunning-Schepers, 1996)), and for cost data a study that allocated total health care costs in the Netherlands in 1988 (39,800 million Dutch guilders, one guilder being about 0.55 US dollar) to age, sex, and disease category (Koopmanschap *et al.,* 1994).

Table I Prevalence of smoking (1A, in %), and Rate Ratios (RR) of smoking for 5 diseases (1B)

IA: prevalence of smoking (%) by gender and age		
Age	**Males**	**Females**
0-14	0	0
15-19	20	20
20-34	39	37
35-49	42	36
50-64	39	27
65+	34	13

IB: RR of smoking for 5 diseases	
Disease	**RR**
Heart	3
Lung ca	10
Stroke	2
Other ca	2
COPD	25

SIX QUESTIONS, SIX METHODS, SIX ANSWERS

Six questions

We examine the impact of smoking on health care costs in six different ways. The first four questions are of a descriptive nature: they are about the annual per capita costs of smokers versus nonsmokers, about the attributable costs, lifetime costs, and population costs. The last two questions are of a different nature: they evaluate the cost-effectiveness of interventions, on a cohort and a population respectively. This distinction is important, because it has implications for the methods.

Question 1

"Are the annual costs of smokers higher or lower than those of nonsmokers?" With the smokers' and nonsmokers' life tables we divided costs in each 5-year age group by the number of years lived by each group, and present the results for the males in Figure I (per capita cost by age). From this Figure two things are apparent: costs rise steeply with age, both for smokers and nonsmokers, but at all ages smokers make higher costs than nonsmokers.

Figure I Annual per capita health care costs for males, by age and smoking status

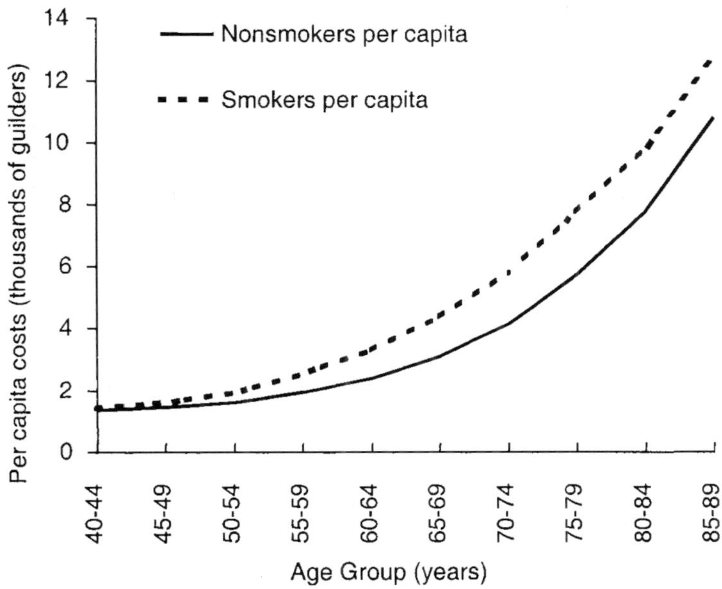

Question 2

"What part of current health care costs is attributable to smoking?". We used the life table with a mixed population of smokers and nonsmokers, and calculated the population attributable risk (PAR) to partition the total cost of the 5 smoking related diseases into a smoking attributable part and a remainder (Table II). The smoking attributable costs are generally lower for women (because at higher ages women smoke less), and range from 12% of disease specific costs for stroke in women to almost 90% for COPD in men. The total smoking attributable costs are 1.88 billion guilders, or about 8% of total health care costs for men, and 2.7% for women.

Table II Population Attributable Costs (millions of guilders, life table population) of smoking by gender and smoking related disease, and as a percentage of disease specific and total costs

	Heart	Stroke	Lung ca	Other ca	COPD	Sum
Males	440	213	174	117	295	1238
Females	173	122	28	91	163	576
			% total			
Males	41.9%	25.6%	76.0%	25.9%	89.4%	7.9%
Females	22.4%	12.0%	61.2%	15.2%	79.6%	2.7%

Question 3

"Are the lifetime costs of smokers higher than those of nonsmokers?" As opposed to questions 1 and 2 this question takes the difference in life expectancy between smokers and nonsmokers into account: the life expectancies at birth for smokers are 69.7 (males) and 75.6 (females), for nonsmokers 77.0 and 81.6 (our life table estimates, which agree very well with the results of Doll (Doll *et al.* 1994)). This implies that at high ages many more nonsmokers than smokers are still alive, for example in our life tables at age 80 about 50% of non-smoking males is still alive, against 21% of smokers.

With the smokers' and nonsmokers' life tables we summed total costs of the life table cohorts over age, and calculated expected life time costs by dividing by the initial size of the cohorts (Bonneux *et al.,* 1998). Women incur over 30% higher lifetime costs than men (Table III), and nonsmokers about 15% higher than smokers. The higher lifetime costs of women are largely due to their longer life expectancy, while the higher costs smokers incur when alive are more than compensated for by their shorter life expectancy.

Table III Lifetime health care costs of smokers and nonsmokers, males and females, Dutch guilders

	Males	Females	Ratio females over males
Smokers	145,400	189,500	1.30
Nonsmokers	166,800	222,800	1.34
Ratio nonsmokers over smokers	1.15	1.18	

Figure II Male life table population costs (millions of guilders) by age, mixed smokers/nonsmokers and nonsmokers

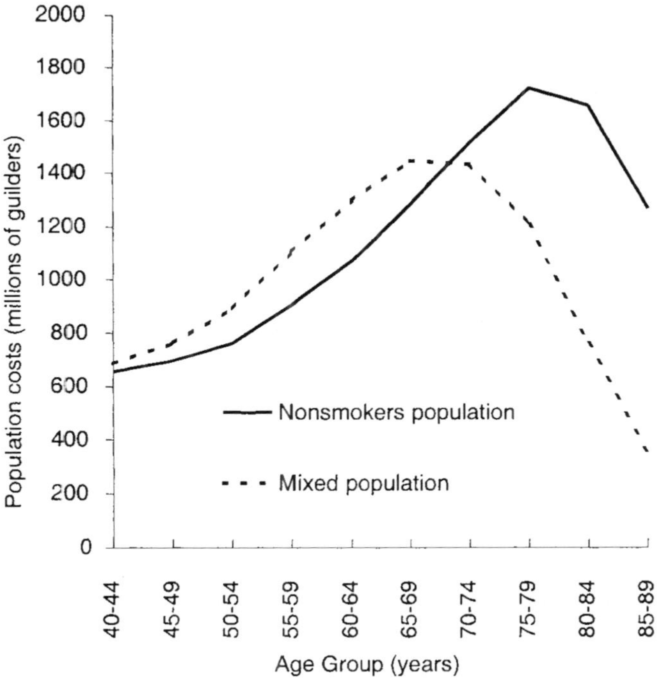

The attributable cost calculation of question 2, probably the most used method (Shultz, Novotny and Rice, 1991) suggests that non-smoking will generate very desirable savings on health care expenditures. But it turns out that sizeable smoking-attributable costs coincide with higher lifetime costs for nonsmokers, therefore the conclusion of potential cost savings does not follow.

Question 4

"Would a population of nonsmokers make more or less medical costs than our current mixed population?" From the mixed and the nonsmokers' life tables we calculated population costs by age and in total. Figure II shows costs by age of the two populations (males only). The differences in population size at high ages have a huge impact: in middle age the mixed population is clearly more expensive due to the higher costs of the smokers, but at higher age the mixed population is so much smaller than the nonsmokers that the lower per capita costs of the latter are outweighed by their larger number.

Table IV *Costs of disease in millions of guilders, life table population with current smoking prevalences, non-smoking life table population, and index mixed=100*

Males	**Heart**	**Stroke**	**Lung ca**	**Other ca**	**COPD**	**Other**	**Total**
Mixed	1050	831	228	453	330	12,720	15,612
Non-smoking	741	855	66	406	47	14,569	16,684
Index	71	103	29	90	14	115	107
Females							
Mixed	772	1019	45	595	204	18,716	21,352
Non-smoking	661	1004	18	528	40	20,025	22,277
Index	86	98	39	89	20	107	104

Table IV shows lifetime costs for both life table populations, broken down by disease. Lung cancer and COPD (the diseases with the highest rate ratios) cost a great deal less in a non-smoking population, heart disease and other cancers considerably less, but stroke is down just a bit (females) or even somewhat more expensive (males). Also more expensive is the large category "other diseases", which makes a non-smoking population on balance 4% (females) and 7% (males) more expensive than the current mixed population.

Change of perspective

So far we have compared smokers and nonsmokers, both with and without taking differences in life expectancy into account. Questions 5 and 6 have a different perspective: they concern the economic evaluation of interventions on smoking prevalence. In other words, they ask which of two alternatives we prefer, doing an intervention versus doing nothing. Another difference, most apparent with question 6, is that after an intervention a transition period occurs: the epidemiological and demographical changes after smoking cessation take time. Therefore whether or not an intervention is financially attractive depends not just on smokers being more expensive or not, but also, given the existence of time preference, on the timing of these future costs and benefits and the choice of discount rate (for simplicitys' sake we ignore the cost of the interventions themselves).

Figure III Difference between non-smoking and smoking cohort health care costs, by gender and discount rate

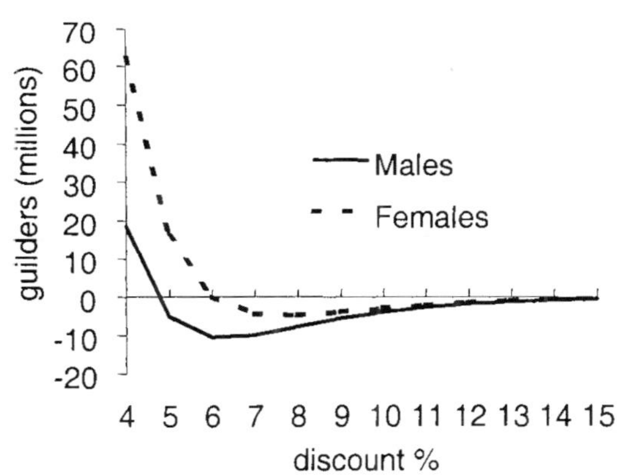

Question 5

"If we could persuade one cohort not to take up smoking, would that be financially attractive?" We interpret the non-smoking and the smoking life tables as cohorts being followed through time until they are extinct. We decide which stream of costs is preferable by discounting future costs to take account of time preference. Figure III shows the difference in costs between the non-smoking and smoking cohorts by discount rate. For a zero discount rate nonsmokers are more expensive by about 2 billion (males) and 3 billion guilders (females): the difference in lifetime costs (Table III) times

100,000 (the size of the cohorts at birth). With increasing discount rate this difference diminishes rapidly, and turns into a nonsmokers' advantage around 4.5% (males) and 6% (females). After reaching a maximum the nonsmokers' advantage subsequently trails off to zero.

This of course makes sense. A nonsmoker cohort incurs lower costs at middle age (because they have less disease) and higher at old age (because more are still alive). Discounting affects costs more as they are made further away in time, which in this case is synonymous with "at older age". With an increasing discount rate first the nonsmokers higher old age costs are discounted away, and the balance tips into their favor, and next also middle age costs are discounted away, leaving the equal costs at younger ages where there are no smokers yet.

Question 6

"Given the current mixed smoker-nonsmoker population, would it be economically attractive when all smokers quit?" This question is of course more relevant from a public health point of view: in the real world we deal with populations, not with single cohorts. A life table can be interpreted as a population, but in such a stationary population interpretation it has no time axis (Shryock and Siegel, 1976). To answer the sixth question we need a dynamic method with separate age and time axes, which can be depicted as a series of linked life tables, one for each point in time. We employed the dynamic population model *Prevent Plus*, which was designed to evaluate risk factor interventions in populations (Barendregt *et al.,* 1998; Gunning-Schepers, Barendregt and Van der Maas 1989).

We set the population at time 0 equal to the mixed smoker-nonsmoker life table population, and did an intervention in year 1 that set smoking-related disease incidences to the level of the nonsmokers. We followed the population for 50 years, and calculated a stream of future health care costs, which differs from the constant costs of "doing nothing" (the "no discounting" line in Figure IV). As a consequence of lower incidence rates prevalence rates start to decline, and so do costs. But at the same time smoking related mortality declines, and the population starts to age. Larger numbers in the higher age groups means upward pressure on health care costs, and in year 5 costs start to rise again, reaching the original level in year 15, and eventually (but after 50 years it is not quite there yet) becoming equal to the difference between smokers and nonsmokers costs of Table IV.

We apply discounting to decide whether the intervention is preferable to doing nothing. Figure IV shows the consequences of discounting the projected costs and benefits by various percentages. It is apparent that discounting, even at a rate as low as 3 percent, has a huge impact, and this impact becomes greater as the costs become more distant in time.

Figure IV Percent change in total health care costs for the male population after smoking cessation. Dynamic analysis, by year of follow up, and for 0, 3, 5 and 10% discount rate

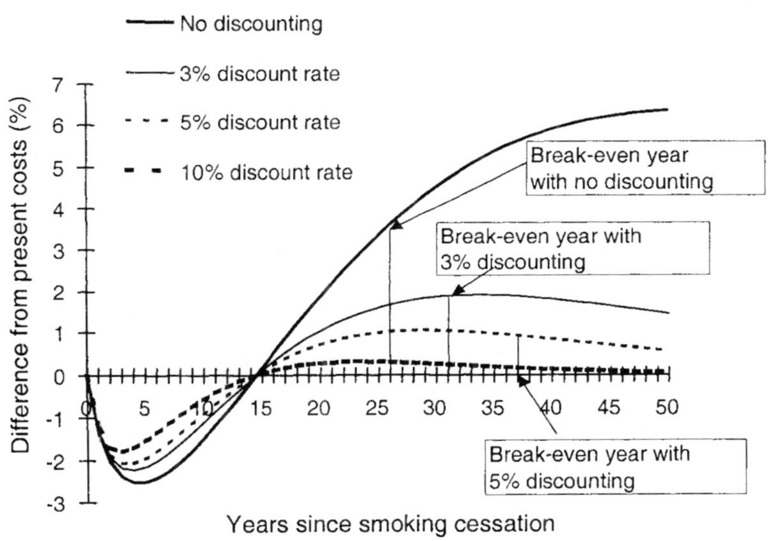

Having all smokers quit becomes economically attractive when the future benefits are larger than the future costs or, in terms of Figure IV, when the area below the X axis is bigger than the area above it. From the Figure it is clear that this depends heavily on the duration of the follow-up time considered and on the discount rate. With a shorter evaluation period and higher discount rates, stopping smoking looks economically more attractive. With a longer evaluation period and lower discount rates, quitting smoking loses its economic advantages. The break-even year, when the initial benefit is exactly balanced by the eventual cost, occurs after 26 years of follow-up when there is no discounting, after 31 years with 3 percent discounting, and after 37 years with 5 percent discounting. At 10 percent discounting, the break-even year occurs after more than 50 years and may not occur at all.

DISCUSSION AND CONCLUSIONS

The question on the economic costs of smoking for the health care sector can be put in many different ways, with answers to match. We have shown that, while smokers have higher per capita costs, and while a sizeable part of health care costs can be attributed to smoking, nonsmokers are more expensive over their lifetime, and that a non-smoking population would be more expensive than the current. And finally: if everybody quits smoking, population costs would initially be lower, but eventually higher, and because of this cost pattern it is economically attractive if everybody quits, given reasonable assumptions on discount rate and time horizon.

Several authors have claimed to estimate lifetime costs, but use a single life table with discounting and are therefore in fact answering question 5 on the intervention on a single cohort (Hodgson, 1992; Manning *et al.,* 1989; Viscusi, 1995). Calculating lifetime costs, however, is a descriptive exercise: there is no intervention and no need to choose between alternative future streams of costs. Discounting is therefore not appropriate, and causes a downward bias in lifetime cost. Because nonsmokers' costs are made at a higher age, their costs are more biased, which in our example will tip the balance and make smokers more expensive for discount rates from 4.5 (males) and 6% (females) and up (Figure III).

Another, but related fallacy is to interpret results from a discounted single cohort analysis as the population cost after an intervention. When a life table is interpreted as a population at one point in time there exists no time axis, only age, and therefore discounting amounts to discounting costs incurred at old age. This fallacy occurred, for example, in a cost-effectiveness study of breast cancer screening (Boer, Oortmarssen, and Koning, 1996; Lindfors and Rosenquist, 1995). It has potentially a huge impact on outcome: the nonsmokers male life table population cost is 16.7 billion (Table IV), and declines to less than 10 billion at 1% "discounting", and to 2.4 billion at 5%.

When does non-smoking save health care money? It is clear that the only right answer to that question is: "It depends". It depends on who is asking the question, and to what purpose. Health insurers, operating in a pay-as-you-go-system, are well excused to charge smokers higher premiums, because smokers have a higher medical consumption, as long as they are alive. A government funded cradle-to-grave-system like the British National Health Service, on the other hand, looks at lifetime costs, which are higher for nonsmokers because they outlive smokers. The state funded US Medicaid system faces higher expenditures because of smoking, since it mostly covers costs up to age 65, and smokers are more expensive in middle age (Figure II). And from a societal point of view, with a suitable choice of time horizon and discount rate, it would save money if all smokers would quit.

How important are the costs of smoking for public health policy? There is clearly a societal interest now that several US states are trying to recoup Medicaid expenditures from tobacco firms. Yet we think that for public health policy the point whether smokers impose a net financial burden or not ought to be of very limited importance indeed. Public health policy is concerned with improving public health, smoking is a major health hazard, so the policy on smoking should be simple and clear: smoking is to be reduced, for example by increasing the tax on tobacco and banning advertisement.

Since we are clearly willing to spend money on added or healthier years of life, the method of choice for evaluations of medical interventions is cost-effectiveness analysis, which generates not a net cost or benefit, but a cost per (quality or disability adjusted) year of life gained. Decision makers then should implement those interventions that, given the budget, yield the highest health revenue (Murray, Kreuser and Whang, 1994). We have no doubt that an effective anti-smoking policy fits the bill.

Yet even a well-designed cost-effectiveness study is marred by inevitable arbitrariness: what costs to include (particularly daunting when indirect costs are considered), which discount rate should be applied (even if consensus existed the rate is arbitrary), and what time horizon to use. Other as yet unsolved problems concern the rationale of societal time preference, and long-term, in particular intergenerational effects (Krahn and Gafni, 1993; West, 1996). While we applaud recent efforts to improve standards of economic evaluation studies, this will not suffice: even if all studies were carried out impeccably fundamental problems with the methodology would still remain (Drummond *et al.*, 1996; Gold *et al.*, 1996; Mason and Drummond, 1995). Health economists should pay more attention to solving these problems to improve a still immature methodology. For the time being, however, conclusions from economic evaluation studies in health care should be interpreted with great caution.

REFERENCES

Barendregt, J.J., Van Oortmarssen, G.J., Van Hout, B.A., Van den Bosch, J.M. and Bonneux, L. (1998), "Coping with Multiple Morbidity in a Life Table, *Mathematical Population Studies,* Vol. 7, No. 1, pp. 29-49.

Barendregt, J.J., Bonneux, L. and Van der Maas, P.J. (1997), "The Health Care Costs of Smoking", *New England Journal of Medicine,* No. 337, pp. 1052-1057.

Boer, R., Van Oortmarssen, G.J. and de Koning, H.J. (1996), "Cost-Effectiveness of Mammography Screening" [Letter], *Journal of the American Medical Association,* Vol. 275, No. 2, pp. 111-112.

Bonneux, L., Barendregt, J.J., Meeter, K., Bonsel, G.J. and Van der Maas, P.J. (1994), "Estimating Clinical Morbidity Due to Ischemic Heart Disease and Congestive Heart Failure", *American Journal of Public Health,* No. 84, pp. 20-28.

Bonneux, L., Barendregt, J.J., Nusselder, W.J. and Van der Maas, P.J. (1998), "Preventing Fatal Diseases Increases Healthcare Costs: Cause Elimination Life Table Approach", *British Medical Journal,* No. 316, pp. 26-29.

Centraal Bureau voor de Statistiek CBS (Published annually), *Overledenen naar doodsoorzaak, leeftijd en geslacht*, serie B1, CBS, Voorburg.

Doll, R., Peto, R., Wheatley, K., Gray, R. and Sutherland, I. (1994), "Mortality in Relation to Smoking: 40 Years' Observations on Male British Doctors", *British Medical Journal,* Vol. 309, No. 6959, pp. 901-911.

Drummond, M.F. and Jefferson, T.O. (1996), "Guidelines for Authors and Peer Reviewers of Economic Submissions to the BMJ. The BMJ Economic Evaluation Working Party", *British Medical Journal,* No. 313, pp. 275-283.

Drummond, M.F., Stoddart, G.L. and Torrance, G.W. (1990), *Methods for the Economic Evaluation of Health Care Programmes*, Oxford Medical Publications, Oxford University Press, Oxford.

Eindhoven Cancer Registry (1991), *Cancer Incidence and Survival 1975-1987 in Southeastern Netherlands*, Comprehensive Cancer Center South, Eindhoven.

Elixhauser, A. (1990), "The Costs of Smoking and the Cost Effectiveness of Smoking-Cessation Programs", *Journal of Public Health Policy,* Vol. 11, No. 2, pp. 218-237.

Foundation of Public Health and Smoking (1993), *Annual Report 1992*, Foundation of Public Health and Smoking, The Hague.

Gold, M.R., Siegel, J.E., Russell, L.B. and Weinstein, M.C. (Eds) (1996), *Cost-Effectiveness in Health and Medicine*, Oxford University Press, New York.

Gunning-Schepers, L.J., Barendregt, J.J. and Van der Maas, P.J. (1989), "Population Interventions Reassessed", *Lancet,* No. I, pp. 479-481.

Hodgson, T.A. (1992), "Cigarette Smoking and Lifetime Medical Expenditures", *Milbank Quarterly,* Vol. 70, No. 1, pp. 81-125.

Kleinbaum, D.G., Kupper, L.L. and Morgenstern, H. (1982), *Epidemiologic Research: Principles and Quantitative Methods,* Lifetime Learning Publications, London.

Koopmanschap, M.A., Van Roijen, L., Bonneux, L., Bonsel, G.J., Rutten, F.F.H. and Van der Maas, P.J. (1994), "Costs of Diseases in an International Perspective", *European Journal of Public Health,* Vol. 4, No. 4, pp. 258-264.

Krahn, M. and Gafni, A. (1993), "Discounting in the Economic Evaluation of Health Care Interventions", *Medical Care,* Vol. 31, No. 5, pp. 403-418.

Leu, R.E. and Schaub, T. (1983), "Does Smoking Increase Medical Care Expenditure?", *Social Science and Medicine,* Vol. 17, No. 23, pp. 1907-1914.

Lindfors, K.K. and Rosenquist, C.J. (1995), "The Cost-Effectiveness of Mammographic Screening Strategies", *Journal of the American Medical Association,* Vol. 274, No. 11, pp. 881-884.

Lippiatt, B.C. (1990), "Measuring Medical Cost and Life Expectancy Impacts of Changes in Cigarette Sales", *Preventive Medicine,* Vol. 19, No. 5, pp. 515-532.

MacKenzie, T.D., Bartecchi, C.E. and Schrier, R.W. (1994), "The Human Costs of Tobacco Use (2)", *New England Journal of Medicine,* Vol. 330, No. 14, pp. 975-980.

Manning, W.G., Keeler, E.B., Newhouse, J.P., Sloss, E.M. and Wasserman, J. (1989), "The Taxes of Sin. Do Smokers and Drinkers Pay their Way?, *Journal of the American Medical Association,* Vol. 261, No. 11, pp. 1604-1609.

Manton, K.G. and Stallard, E. (1988), "Chronic Disease Modelling", in: Baily, N.T.J. (Ed.), *Mathematics in Medicine,* Vol. 2, Charles Griffin & Company Ltd, London.

Mason, J. and Drummond, M. (1995), "Reporting Guidelines for Economic Studies", *Health Economics,* No 4, pp. 85-94.

Murray, C.J., Kreuser, J. and Whang, W. (1994), "Cost-Effectiveness Analysis and Policy Choices: Investing in Health Systems", *Bulletin of the World Health Organisation,* Vol. 72, No. 4, pp. 663-674.

Niessen, L.W., Barendregt, J.J., Bonneux, L. and Koudstaal, P.J. (1993), "Stroke Trends in an Aging Population", *Stroke,* No. 24, pp. 931-939.

Schoen, R. (1987), "Modelling Multigroup Populations", in: Land, K.C. (Ed.), *The Plenum Series on Demographic Methods and Population Analysis,* Plenum Press, New York and London.

Shryock, H.S. and Siegel, J.S. (1976), "The Methods and Materials of Demography", condensed edition, in: Stockwell, E.G. (Ed.), Academic Press, Inc., Orlando.

Shultz, J.M., Novotny, T.E. and Rice, D.P. (1991), "Quantifying the Disease Impact of Cigarette Smoking with SAMMEC II Software", *Public Health Reports,* Vol. 106, No. 3, pp. 326-333.

Van de Mheen, P.J. and Gunning-Schepers, L.J. (1996), "Differences Between Studies in Reported Relative Risks Associated with Smoking: An Overview", *Public Health Reports,* No. 111, pp. 420-426.

Van Weel, C., Van den Bosch, J.M., Van den Hoogen, H.J.M. and Smits, A.J.A. (1987), "Development of Respiratory Illness in Childhood: A Longitudinal Study in General Practice", *Journal of the Royal College of General Practitioners,* No. 37, pp. 404-408.

Viscusi, W.K. (1995), "Cigarette Taxation and the Social Consequences of Smoking", in: Poterba J. (Ed.), *Tax Policy and the Economy,* National Bureau of Economic Research, Washington.

West, R.R. (1996), "Discounting the Future: Influence of the Economic Model", *Journal of Epidemiology and Community Health,* No. 50, pp. 239-244.

APPENDIX

Population Attributable Risk

The Population Attributable Risk (PAR, also known as Etiologic Fraction), the proportion of the total number of cases of a disease that can be attributed to smoking, is calculated by:

$$PAR = \frac{p(R - 1)}{p(R - 1) + 1} \tag{1}$$

with p smoking prevalence (proportion), R the rate ratio, and R-1 a measure for the excess risk of smokers (Kleinbaum, Kupper and Morgenstern, 1982).

Three life tables

We do not have direct observations on the difference in epidemiology between smokers and nonsmokers, and therefore use rate ratios to differentiate between smokers and nonsmokers incidence. We first estimate for the total population (so smokers and nonsmokers combined) disease specific prevalences and survival, using disease and age specific incidence and mortality rates as input (Barendregt *et al.,* 1998). We assume the survival for all diseases to be equal for smokers and nonsmokers. Using the observation that the observed population incidence is a weighted average of the higher smokers and the lower nonsmokers incidence, we estimate disease specific incidence for smokers and nonsmokers from the average population incidence, the rate ratio on incidence for smokers, and smoking prevalence by:

$$i = p i^1 + (1 - p) i^0 \tag{2}$$

and:

$$i^1 = i^0 R \tag{3}$$

Substituting eq (3) in (2) we can write the incidence of the nonsmokers as:

$$i^0 = \frac{i}{pR + 1 - p} \tag{4}$$

Where:

i: average incidence rate of disease;

i^0: incidence rate of disease for nonsmokers, i^1 for smokers;

p: prevalence of smoking;

R: rate ratio on incidence of disease, given exposure to smoking.

With these smoking specific incidences and disease specific survival we then estimate separate life tables for smokers and nonsmokers.

Discounting

A decision maker is confronted with two investment projects that differ both in timing of future costs and revenues as in amounts. The problem for the decision maker is which project, if any, to choose. To be able to make this decision the two streams are converted to Present Values (PV's) using:

$$PV = \sum_{t=0}^{t=t_H} \frac{P_t}{(1+r)^t} \tag{5}$$

Where:

t: time, with $t=0$ the present.

t_H: time horizon of evaluation.

P_t: amount of cost or benefit at time t.

r: interest rate.

The decision maker maximises profit when he picks the project with the highest PV, and never chooses a project with a negative PV (because that project would make a loss). Note that there are two unknowns in equation 5: the time horizon t_H and the interest rate r. While in a commercial enterprise obvious values for these unknowns may exist, like amortisation period and market rate of interest, this is less obvious for medical interventions.

6

NEW GUIDELINES FOR ESTIMATING THE ECONOMIC COSTS OF SMOKING, AND RESULTS FROM CANADA

ERIC SINGLE

There is a strong interest in many countries regarding the development of scientifically valid, credible estimates of the economic costs of tobacco as well as other forms of substance abuse. The costs of drugs is an issue of key interest to stakeholders, policy makers and the media. Knowledge of the costs of resources associated with drug abuse informs decisions related to funding and to interventions which are designed to reduce abuse. Relatively few countries have attempted to estimate the costs of substance abuse. Such estimates are fraught with methodological difficulties resulting in widely varying estimates.

In this presentation I will briefly describe a set of guidelines recently developed to estimate the social and economic costs of substance abuse generally, and tobacco use in particular (Single, 1996a), and I will then describe the results of a study estimating the costs of tobacco use in Canada (Single, 1996b; 1998; in press).

INTERNATIONAL GUIDELINES FOR ESTIMATING THE COSTS OF SUBSTANCE ABUSE

In May 1994 an international symposium was held in Banff, Canada, to discuss the issues involved in estimating the social and economic costs of substance abuse, and to seek a consensus on the most appropriate model. The purpose of the meeting was to explore the feasibility of establishing an internationally acceptable common methodology for estimating the costs of drugs. The symposium in Banff brought together persons with experience and expertise in dealing with the issues of costs estimation. A working group was formed to explore the potential for developing guidelines on estimating the economic costs of substance abuse, consisting of myself, David Collins, Brian Easton, Rick Harwood, Helen Lapsley and Alan Maynard. These guidelines were drafted and finalised at a second International Symposium held in Montebello, Quebec, in 1996 (Single, 1996a).

The guidelines begin with a discussion of the purposes of cost estimates. Estimates of the social and economic costs of substance abuse serve many purposes:

- First, economic cost estimates are frequently used to argue that policies on tobacco and other psychoactive substances should be given a high priority on the public policy agenda. The public is entitled to a quality standard against which individual cost estimation studies can be assessed. Without such a standard there will be a tendency by the advocates for each social problem to overbid, adding in additional items to make their concern a suitably high (even exaggerated) number.

- Second, cost estimates help to appropriately target specific problems and policies. It is important to know which psychoactive substances involve the greatest economic costs. For example, the recent study by Collins and Lapsley (1991) concluded that the costs of alcohol and tobacco far exceeds the social costs from illicit drugs in Australia, thus focusing greater attention on public policy towards the licit drugs. Would a similar conclusion be reached in other countries? The specific types of cost may also draw our attention to specific areas which need public attention, or where specific measures may be effective.

- Third, economic cost studies help to identify information gaps, research needs and desirable refinements to national statistical reporting systems.

- Last but not least, the development of improved estimates of the costs of substance abuse offers the potential, although generally not yet realised,

> to provide baselines measures to determine which policies and programmes are the most effective in reducing the harm associated with tobacco and other drug use. International comparisons of reliable cost estimates could provide important indicators of the effectiveness of national policies. Are the costs of smoking higher in less restrictive societies? Other things being equal, is there less smoking in countries where a greater proportion of the costs are borne by the individual? Ultimately, cost estimates could be used to construct social cost functions for optimal tax policy and national target setting.

The next part of the guidelines presents "a layperson's guide to economic cost estimation". In brief, the study of the economic costs of problems associated with the use of psychoactive substances is described as (1) a type of cost-of-illness study (2) in which the impact of substance abuse on the material welfare of a society is estimated by examining (3) the *social costs* of resources expended for treatment, prevention, research and law enforcement, plus (4) losses of production due to increased morbidity and mortality, plus (5) some measure for the quality of life years lost, relative to a counterfactual scenario in which there is no substance abuse. Each part of this statement is discussed in detail. The concept of opportunity cost is described, and the importance of the counterfactual scenario in the COI framework noted. It is argued that to be credible, estimates of the costs of substance abuse must be clear with regard to what constitutes a cost, who bears these costs and the boundaries which should be placed on the economic ramifications of negative impacts. Differences between the demographic approach developed by Collins and Lapsley and the more common human capital approach are also discussed. Finally, it is noted that much of the appeal and desire for economic cost estimates of tobacco and other psychoactive substances may unfortunately be based on confusion with other types of economic analyses. While useful and relevant to policy decisions, COI studies are *not* studies of avoidable costs, they are not studies of budgetary impact nor are they cost-benefit analyses. The differences between COI studies and these types of economic analyses are described in this "layperson's guide".

Section 3 presents a framework for the development of cost estimates. The major principle underlying the decision regarding which costs to include is the robustness of the estimates, which is in turn dependent on the availability of data. A matrix of costs to consider is presented. As applied in the Canadian setting, these costs are categorised as:

1. Direct health care costs, including treatment in general and psychiatric hospitals, co-morbidity costs, ambulance services, residential care, treatment agencies, ambulatory care (physician fees and other professional services), prescription drugs and other health care costs (e.g., household help, rehabilitation equipment).

2. Direct losses associated with the workplace, including an attributable portion of Employee Assistance Programs (EAPs) and other health programs, as well the cost of drug testing in the workplace.

3. Direct administrative costs for transfer payments, such as social welfare, workers' compensation and other programs.

4. Direct costs for prevention, research, training and averting behaviour costs.

5. Direct law enforcement costs, including an attributable portion of police, court, corrections and customs costs.

6. Other direct costs such as fire damage, traffic accident damage and reduced property values in drug ridden communities.

7. Indirect costs: productivity losses due to lower productivity resulting from substance-related disease (e.g., absenteeism), productivity losses due to premature mortality and productivity losses due to crime and crime careers.

Section 4 of the guidelines discusses conceptual and methodological issues in the application of the cost framework. The purpose is not to advocate a particular approach, but to describe alternatives and discuss the advantages and disadvantages of each approach for particular purposes. The following issues are discussed:

Definition of costs

The economic definition of cost employed in the COI is based on the concept of alternative uses for scarce resources, known as opportunity cost. Focus is placed on the tangible social costs of substance abuse. The social costs are the sum of the private and external costs after adjusting for transfers within society. In general, the major direct costs are external costs (i.e. those costs borne by persons other than the abuser). In many studies, the costs imposed on the abuser's family are generally included. Although certain minor internal costs are often included (such as the private costs of drugs for treatment or the costs of property damage due to tobacco-related fires), in COI studies the major direct costs considered are external costs born by persons other than the user. The costs of purchasing drugs to the users are not generally included. Nor are transfer payments, such as welfare payments to persons disabled by substance abuse (although administrative costs are included).

Definition of abuse

COI studies attempt to quantify the costs of problems associated with the misuse of psychoactive substances, rather than just those costs associated with physical dependence or heavy use. This is obviously a much less important issue for tobacco than it is for alcohol and illicit drugs, since virtually all smokers are dependent. Drug abuse encompasses any drug use which involves a social cost additional to the resource costs of the provision of that drug. Thus, the costs of "abuse" include costs associated with moderate levels of use if such use incurs social costs to the community.

Causality

Many adverse consequences arise from multiple causes in which substance abuse may or may not play a role. The first step is to obtain information that provides a plausible basis for attributing some proportion of the cases associated with the particular negative consequence to substance abuse (the attributable or etiologic fraction). The extent to which a particular consequence can be attributed to the use of drugs varies according to setting, both for epidemiological reasons and due to variations in the institutional arrangements for dealing with adverse consequences. Thus, for example, the apparent proportion of lung cancer which can be attributed to smoking is influenced not only by the relative risk of developing lung cancer at given levels of consumption and the rate and patterns of smoking in a society, but also by the incidence of lung cancer not caused by smoking, the availability of treatment and the reporting practices of health authorities. The most complete and recent reviews of the appropriate etiologic fractions for alcohol, tobacco and illicit drugs (English *et al.*, 1995; Shultz *et al.*, 1991a; Shultz *et al.*, 1991b; Fox *et al.*, 1995) may be used to identify substance-related disorders and studies bearing upon the etiologic fractions. The etiologic fractions from these reviews must be adjusted to take differences in prevalence of use in a particular society into account, and in some instances, etiologic fractions for acute consequences (e.g. fire damage and injuries attributable to smoking) may have to be adjusted on the basis of special investigations.

Welfare costs

The only welfare costs included in the COI framework are administrative costs. Welfare payments to users and their dependants are not included on the basis that such expenditures are simply pecuniary costs (i.e. transfer payments). This is done to avoid double counting of costs. If a person previously in the workforce receives welfare benefits as a result smoking-related sickness, it would be inaccurate to include both the productivity loss and the cost of welfare benefits.

Treatment of non-workforce mortality and morbidity

The valuation of production lost as a result of substance use is generally the value of wages forgone, on the basis that wages are equal to the worker's productivity. However, this approach to costing is not entirely satisfactory because it does not assign any value to the unemployed, the retired or those persons outside the paid workforce, since they do not earn wages. The guidelines note some alternative approaches to deal with this issue. For example, an investigator may assume that all people of working age who are not in the workforce (i.e. employed or seeking employment) are providing non-market services. This implies that the sickness or death of such people involves withdrawal of others from the workforce to maintain the supply of non-market services. For example, the death of a non-working mother of pre-school or school age children means that those children must be looked after by someone else, who thus becomes unavailable for employment. In the Canadian study, the productive value lost due to the mortality or morbidity takes into account the value of housework.

Use of gross vs. net costs

The use of alcohol, tobacco and illicit drugs involves benefits as well as costs. Thus, for example, smoking is associated with increased risk of many health disorders but smoking is also associated with decreased levels of Parkinson's Disease. For causes of disease and death where use of a psychoactive substance has beneficial effects, the investigator may choose to present a net estimate of morbidity and mortality which become the basis of the economic cost estimates, or he or she may choose instead to present only a gross estimate of the cases caused by misuse without subtracting out the number of cases prevented by use. The rationale for only including gross costs is that estimates of the costs of alcohol, tobacco and illicit drugs should not include partial consideration of benefits.[1] However, it is recommended that if gross estimates of morbidity and mortality are used, the number of cases prevented by the use of a particular substance should be tabulated and presented, so that comparisons may be drawn to the results of studies which report net rather than gross costs.

Avoidable costs

The economic cost estimates in the COI framework do not indicate the amount of money and life years which could realistically be saved via effective government and social policy and programming. The counterfactual situation is one in which there are no problems associated with the use of psychoactive substances. This counterfactual situation is hypothetical and generally not realisable under any circumstances. Thus the estimated costs include both avoidable and unavoidable costs. Even if completely effective policies could be found with no appreciable costs for enforcement, treatment and prevention programming, implementation would not be instantaneous and there would still be lingering adverse consequences from past use of the psychoactive substances.

Importance of intangible costs

The guidelines are careful to point out that intangible costs are viewed as significant even if they cannot be estimated in dollar terms. The major intangible costs of substance use to be considered in estimating the costs of substance abuse are caused by death, pain, suffering and bereavement. Because it is difficult to place a value upon intangible costs, the temptation exists to ignore them. However, to do so may be misleading. Consider, for example, the costs of smoking. A high proportion of tobacco-related deaths occur around or beyond the age of retirement, in which case the community receives a tangible economic benefit because the forgone consumption of retirees may exceed their forgone production. Consideration of tangible

---

[1] Furthermore, as was shown with regard to alcohol, cases caused by substance misuse may more often involve relatively young persons compared with cases prevented. Thus, subtracting the lives saved from the lives lost would lead to underestimation of the years of potential life lost and, consequently, the economic costs associated with premature death due to substance abuse.

costs and benefits alone might lead to the incorrect conclusion that smoking benefits the community by leading to the premature death of thousands of people. The conclusion would obviously be false – people beyond working age do not cease to be of value to the society simply because they cease to work[2].

The guidelines conclude with a brief discussion of future directions, with particular attention to the expansion of economic cost studies to developing countries, and the implications of these guidelines to research agendas and data collection systems. These guidelines provide a framework rather than a rigorous methodology to be applied in every situation. It is recognised that there will not be sufficient data in many countries to implement the recommendations in this document. However, in many countries it will be possible to develop reasonable estimates for some, if not most, of the costs associated with substance abuse. It is hoped that these guidelines will help facilitate the development of more economic cost studies and enhance the comparability of such estimates.

The guidelines are only a tentative first step in a process aimed at developing more reliable and credible estimates of the costs of substance abuse. The next step in this process will be to apply the recommended procedures in new national and regional studies. This in turn should lead to further refinements to these guidelines. The long-term goal is to move from cost estimation to cost effectiveness analyses, and eventually to cost-benefit analyses of substance abuse policies and programmes.

THE COSTS OF SMOKING IN CANADA: RESULTS FROM A RECENT STUDY UTILISING THE GUIDELINES

Utilising these guidelines, a major study was undertaken to estimate morbidity, mortality and economic costs attributable to substance abuse in Canada in 1992. Only the results regarding tobacco will be reported here.

---

[2]While the study does not include a dollar value on the intangible aspects of life years lost due to substance abuse, it does estimate the numbers of life-years lost for each major type of substance (Single, Robson *et al.*, 1996). This will permit those who wish to do so to estimate these costs in dollar terms, using the "willingness to pay" method of valuation (Collins and Lapsley, 1991).

The first step in estimating the costs of tobacco is to estimate the number of deaths and hospitalisations attributable to smoking. The methodology is described elsewhere (Single, 1996b; Single *et al.*, in press). Briefly put, information on relative risks for different causes of disease and death (using ICD-9 categories) are estimated from meta-analyses (particularly Shultz *et al.*, 1991b; Fox *et al.*, 1995; and English *et al.*, 1995). Controlling for age and gender, pooled estimates of relative risk are combined with prevalence data to generate "etiologic fractions" or attributable proportions of the total deaths and hospitalisations for those causes. These are then applied to reported numbers of deaths and hospitalisations due to each cause (controlling again for age and gender).

The total number of tobacco-related deaths in Canada is estimated to be 33,498 in 1992 and the total number of years of potential life lost is estimated at 495,640. More than one third (35%) of tobacco-related deaths are due to lung cancer. There were 208,095 hospital separations and more than 3 million hospitalisation days (3,024,265) resulting from tobacco-related causes in Canada in 1992. Tobacco-related causes account for 17% of total mortality, 16% of total years of potential life lost, 6% of all hospitalisations and 7% of all hospital days for any cause in Canada for 1992[3].

Tobacco accounts for more than $9.5 billion in costs to the Canadian economy, or $340 per capita. This is more than one half (51.8%) of the total substance abuse costs. Lost productivity due to morbidity and premature mortality accounts for more than $6.82 billion of these costs and direct health care costs due to smoking account for $2.68 billion in costs. Time does not permit a detailed accounting of these costs, which is available in the study report (Single, 1996b; Single *et al.*, in press). In terms of the major cost categories noted earlier, the economic impact of tobacco use is

[3] The use of tobacco does not prevent nearly as many deaths or hospitalizations as it causes. It is estimated that 356 deaths were prevented (237 males and 119 females) mainly due to the beneficial effects of smoking on Parkinson's Disease (295 deaths prevented) and endometrial cancer (59 deaths prevented). The number of hospitalizations prevented by tobacco use is estimated at 3,089 (1,196 for males and 1,871 for females) with a total hospitalization days of 146,527 (100,904 for males and 45,623 for females).

estimated as follows:

- Health care costs: $ 2.675 billion.
- Workplace prevention: $ 5.5 million.
- Prevention, research, training: $ 48 million.
- Other direct costs such as fire damage: $17.1 million.
- Productivity losses due to mortality and morbidity: $6.818 billion.

Comparisons with other studies

The findings regarding the economic costs of smoking in this study are similar to the findings of Rice *et al.* (1986) in 1980 in the U.S. The estimates are somewhat lower than Collishaw and Myers (1984), probably reflecting the decrease in smoking prevalence between 1979 and 1992. The findings are considerably higher than those of Raynauld and Vidal (1992) in Canada in 1986, who only examined external costs and did not include lost productivity due to premature mortality. The estimated costs of tobacco are considerably higher than those of Collins and Lapsley (1996) for Australia in 1992, who used a different methodology to estimate productivity costs.

The estimated number of tobacco deaths is 18% lower that the 41,100 deaths due to tobacco for 1991 estimated by Makamaski-Illing and Kaiserman (1995) using the SAMMEC attributable fractions. The differences may in part be due to different referent years, but most of the difference is due to the use of different attributable fractions. For example, the risk ratio for lung cancer for male smokers according to SAMMEC (Shultz *et al.*, 1991b) is 22 compared to the estimate of 13 used in this study, based on English *et al.* (1995). Although the SAMMEC estimate is based on one of the largest studies (DHHS, 1989), the estimate risk ratios used in this study are based on ten studies in addition to the study cited in the SAMMEC estimate. As lung cancer accounts for the largest proportion of deaths associated with tobacco use, this difference accounts in part for the lower estimated tobacco-related mortality.

Sensitivity analyses

Sensitivity analyses were conducted to examine the extent to which the results are affected by the choice of particular methods for estimating cost components. Specifically, the impact of weighting hospitalisation costs by diagnosis and the use of alternative discount rates are examined[4].

With regard to the first sensitivity analysis, prior studies of the economic costs of substance abuse have generally used a mean cost per hospital day to estimate hospitalisation costs. This is typically a matter of necessity, as diagnosis-specific cost information is not available. However, it is well known that particular disorders involve considerably higher (or lower) costs. At issue is whether the use of a mean hospitalisation cost biases the results in one direction or the other, leading to an underestimation or overestimation of such costs. A special analysis found that controlling for differential costs for different diagnoses would have resulted in cost estimates which are 14% higher for tobacco[5]. Thus, estimates of hospitalisation costs attributable to tobacco use do vary when weighted according to the specific diagnosis.

The other sensitivity analysis concerned the use of alternative discount rates to estimate lost productivity. Estimates of the value of lost productivity due to premature mortality are strongly influenced by the choice of the discount rate used to compute the present value of future earnings. The study report presents the estimated productivity losses due to premature mortality using discount rates of 4%, 5%, 6% and 10%. The costs reported as the main estimate in this study are based on a 6% discount rate[6]. The total estimated value of lifetime earnings of persons who die prematurely from tobacco-related conditions ranges from $5.00 billion using a discount rate of 10% to $8.06 billion using a discount rate of 4%. Thus, the choice of discount rate makes a considerable difference to the estimated productivity losses, and consequently to the total estimated costs of tobacco use.

---

[4]A further sensitivity analysis was conducted regarding the use of alternative consumption measures but this only applied to estimating the costs of alcohol misuse.

[5]Taking diagnosis into account made a much smaller difference for alcohol and illicit drugs.

[6]Assuming a 1% annual increase in productivity (Xie *et al.*, 1996), this represents an effective discount rate of 5%.

CONCLUSIONS OF THE COST STUDY

The first and foremost conclusion of this study is that tobacco use exacts a considerable toll to Canadian society in terms of illness, injury, death and economic costs. Tobacco is perhaps the leading preventable cause of death in Canada today and it accounts for huge costs to the health care system and to the economy in general.

While these figures underscore the toll which tobacco use takes on Canadian society, a second general conclusion of this study is that mortality and morbidity attributable to tobacco and other forms of substance abuse are nonetheless lower than prior estimates indicated. The estimate of mortality attributable to tobacco is 18% lower than previous estimates. The lower estimated tobacco-attributed morbidity and mortality in this study is largely due to the use of pooled estimates from several studies on the relative risks of smoking, rather than relying exclusively on one study.

Sensitivity analyses were conducted on the impact of weighting hospitalisation costs by diagnosis, the use of alternative prevalence measures and the use of alternative discount rates. It is further concluded that the choice of discount rate makes a considerable difference to the estimated productivity losses, and consequently to the total estimated costs of substance abuse. Weighting hospitalisation costs by diagnosis does not effect the costs estimates as much, but it appears that the use of a mean hospitalisation cost may result in underestimation of hospitalisation costs attributable to tobacco use.

The Canadian study attempts to provide up-to-date, detailed estimates of the economic costs of substance abuse in Canada. It is hoped that it will stimulate further research into the economic ramifications of tobacco use and other forms of substance misuse. In addition to periodically refining and updating of cost estimates, more studies are also required on the impact of substance abuse to government budgets, as well as the benefits associated with psychoactive substances. The eventual goal is to develop a sufficient body of knowledge to facilitate cost benefit analyses of specific policies and: programmes to prevent substance abuse.

REFERENCES

Canadian Institute on Health Information (CIHI) (1994/95), *Resource Intensity Weights – Summary of Methodology,* CIHI, Ottawa.

Collins, D. and Lapsley, H. (1991), *Estimating the Economic Costs of Drug Abuse in Australia,* National campaign Against Drug Abuse Monograph No. 15.

Collins, D. and Lapsley, H. (1996), *The Social Costs of Drug Abuse in Australia in 1988 and 1992,* Commonwealth Department of Human Services and Health, Canberra.

Collishaw, N. and Myers, G. (1984), "Dollar Estimates of the Consequences of Tobacco Use in Canada, 1979", *Canadian Journal of Public Health,* Vol. 75, No. 3, pp. 192-199.

English, D., Holman, D., Milne, E., Winter, M., Hulse, G., Codde, G., Bower, C., Corti, B., De Klerk, C., Lewin, G., Knuiman, M., Kurinczuk, J. and Ryan, G. (1995), *The Quantification of Drug Caused Morbidity and Mortality in Australia, 1992,* Commonwealth Department of Human Services and Health, Canberra.

Fox, K., Merrill, J., Chang, H. and Califano, J. (1995), "Estimating the Costs of Substance Abuse to the Medicaid Hospital Care Program", *American Journal of Public Health,* Vol. 85, No. 1, pp. 48-54.

Makamaski-Illing, E. and Kaiserman, M. (1995), "Mortality Attributable to Tobacco Use in Canada and its Regions –1991", *Canadian Journal of Public Health,* Vol 86, pp. 257-265.

Raynauld, A. and Vidal, J.P. (1992), "Smokers' Burden on Society: Myth and Reality in Canada", *Canadian Public Policy,* Vol. 18, pp. 300-317.

Rice, D.P., Hodgson, T.A., Sinsheimer, O., Browner, W. and Kopstein, A.N. (1986), "The Economic costs of the health effects of smoking, 1984", *The Millbank Quaterly*, Vol. 64, No. 4, pp. 489-547.

Shultz, J., Rice, D., Parker, D., Goodman, R., Stroh, G. and Chalmers, N. (1991a), "Quantifying the Disease Impact of Alcohol With ARDI Software", *Public Health Reports,* Vol. 106, No. 4, pp. 443-450.

Shultz, J., Novotny, T. and Rice, D. (1991b), "Quantifying the Disease Impact of Cigarette Smoking With SAMMEC II Software", *Public Health Reports,* Vol. 106, pp. 326-333.

Single, E., Collins, D., Easton, B., Harwood, H., Lapsley, H. and Maynard, A. (1996a), *International Guidelines on Estimating the Costs of Substance Abuse*, Canadian Centre on Substance Abuse, Ottawa.

Single, E., Robson, L., Xie, X. and Rehm, J. (1996b), *The Costs of Substance Abuse in Canada*, Canadian Centre on Substance Abuse, Ottawa.

Single, E., Robson, L., Xie, X. and Rehm, J. (1998), "The Economic Costs of Alcohol, Tobacco and Illicit Drugs in Canada, 1992", *Addiction*, Vol. 93, pp. 983-998.

Single, E., Robson, L., Xie, X. and Rehm, J. (in press), "Morbidity and Mortality Attributable to Substance Abuse in Canada", *American Journal of Public Health.*

U.S. Department of Health and Human Services (DHHS) (1989), *Reducing the Health Consequences of Smoking: 25 Years of Progress. A Report of the Surgeon General,* DHHS Publication No. (CDC) 89-8411.

Xie, S., Rehm, J., Single, E. and Robson, L. (1996), *The Economic Costs of Alcohol, Tobacco and Illicit Drug Abuse in Ontario, 1992"*, Addiction Research Foundation, Toronto.

COUNTRY STUDIES

7

ECONOMIC CONSEQUENCES OF SMOKING IN FINLAND

MARKKU PEKURINEN

BACKGROUND

This paper reports results of an updated analysis of the economic consequences of smoking in Finland. The original study was carried out at the end of the 1980s to help health policy makers design an economic policy towards smoking (Pekurinen, 1991).

Finland had experienced dramatic changes in her tobacco policy during the 1970s and the 1980s. In the 1970s Finland had adopted a medical, strongly administrative and highly successful approach towards smoking. Television advertising of tobacco products was banned in 1971. The Tobacco Act of 1977 imposed major restrictions on all types of advertising and smoking in public places. It was one of the first attempts in the whole world to establish a comprehensive strategy to reduce smoking by legislation.

Towards the end of the 1980s economic paradigm changed and health policy makers faced increasing pressures from the treasury, commerce and industry to defend their health case on strict economic grounds.

TRENDS IN TOBACCO CONSUMPTION

Consumption of tobacco products increased rapidly in Finland after the Second World War. The growth stopped in 1976 and fell by 15% due to excessive price increases, legislative actions and other factors, and remained virtually unchanged for the next 15 years. Successive increases in the real price of tobacco and the severe economic recession, coupled with a significant fall in real disposable income, caused a downward trend in tobacco consumption since the early 1990s (Figure I).

The prevalence of smoking in the adult population has changed in a manner similar to other developed countries. The proportion of smoking males has decreased since the 1960s to about 30%. Smoking among females has become more popular, and the proportion of smoking women has gradually increased to about 20% (Statistics Finland, 1998).

AIM OF THE STUDY

The primary aim of the original study was to see if there was a case for government intervention on the tobacco markets in Finland at the end of the 1980s on other than purely paternalistic grounds. In order to facilitate this, four tasks were pursued.

The first task was to outline analytical economic frameworks that would be suitable to explore the economic problems related to smoking. The second task was to outline broad welfare effects of most important policy options to influence smoking, e.g. taxation, health education, restrictions on availability of tobacco and improvements in risks technology. The third task was to evaluate empirically the health and economic consequences of smoking in order to highlight the magnitude of the likely problem. The fourth and final task was to evaluate the effectiveness of various policy-measures (taxation, legislation, etc) by carrying out extensive econometric demand analyses.

The aim of this paper is to re-evaluate the economic case for government intervention on the tobacco markets in Finland at the end of the 1990s. In order to do this, we shall analyse the health, resource, economic and financial consequences of smoking in Finland in 1995 and compare them to 1987 figures, which was the year of the original study.

Figure I Annual consumption and the real price of tobacco products in Finland 1960-1997

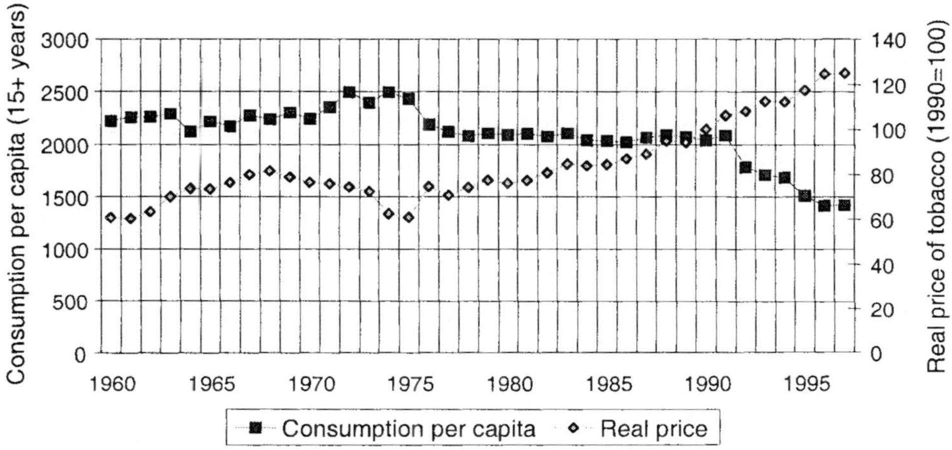

ANALYTICAL FRAMEWORK

When we start exploring economic consequences of smoking, particularly the costs, one of the most important decisions to take is to choose the analytical economic framework for the study. We have at least five options here (Table I).

The medical model is most commonly used to evaluate the costs of smoking (e.g. Pekurinen, 1991; Rice *et al.*, 1986). The obvious problem with the medical model is that it ignores the consumption benefits of smoking. At the other end of the spectrum we have the traditional economic model which allows for the consumption benefits, but assumes smokers to be fully informed and ignores the addictive nature of tobacco.

Somewhere between these two extremes we may outline at least three modifications to the traditional economic model and allow for consumer benefits and for various degrees of incomplete information and dependency (Atkinson and Meade, 1974; Markandya and Pearce, 1989; Pekurinen, 1991).

Table I highlights the five analytical models used in the study and indicates how the models were defined in terms of consumer benefits, incomplete information and dependency. It also shows in each case, which costs were thought to be relevant in defining a policy.

Few points are worth noting in Table I. Unperceived costs reflect those private costs, which fall on smokers, but that they are unaware of. In case smokers are fully informed and addicted (modified economic model 3), these costs reflect perceived private costs for those smokers who would like to give up smoking, but can not do it due to addiction.

Disbenefits due to addiction reflect the welfare loss suffered by smokers who would like to give up smoking, but can not do it due to addiction.

Medical model and modified economic model 1 cover the same cost items, but they view consumption benefits differently. The medical model does not acknowledge any benefits while the economic model does.

Table I Alternative policy relevant costing models used in the study (Pekurinen, 1991)

	Economic model	**Modified economic model 1**	**Modified economic model 2**	**Modified economic model 3**	**Medical model**
CONSUMERS					
Fully informed	Yes	No	No	Yes	No
Addicted	No	No	Yes	Yes	No
CONSUMER BENEFITS FROM SMOKING	Yes	Yes	Yes	Yes	No
POLICY RELEVANT COSTS					
External costs	Yes	Yes	Yes	Yes	Yes
Unperceived costs	No	Yes	Yes	Yes	Yes
Disbenefits due to addiction	No	No	Yes	Yes	No

SOCIAL AND EXTERNAL COSTS

Social costs of smoking are the total costs of smoking to the whole of society. Part of these costs are private or internal costs that are borne by smokers themselves. Part of the social costs are external costs that smokers impose on nonsmokers. External costs are the relevant costs for designing policy towards smoking.

External costs can be viewed from two angles. They may be evaluated either from the institutional perspective (institutional externalities) or from the nonsmokers perspective (final externalities). Institutional external costs represent the costs falling directly to other parties or institutions other than smokers as consumers, such as the state, local authorities, social insurance and firms.

Final external costs are the true external costs that fall on nonsmokers (vs. smokers) and allow for the fact that smokers themselves pay and finance part of the services and expenditures they incur. Figure II illustrates the difference between these two types of external costs.

ESTIMATION METHODOLOGY

The approach used to analyse policy relevant economic consequences of smoking has been described in detail elsewhere (Pekurinen, 1991). Here we shall briefly outline the basic methodology. Firstly, we defined and estimated the social costs of smoking using the traditional cross-sectional cost-of-illness methodology (e.g. Hodgson and Meiners, 1982). After that, we estimated the various financial consequences of smoking. Finally, we estimated the external and other policy-relevant costs with various assumptions about addiction and imperfect information as outlined in Table I.

Table II gives an idea of the direct and indirect cost and benefit items, as well as expenditure and revenue items identified and estimated in the study. As will be noted, two types of economic analyses were performed. One focused on the real economic consequences of smoking (i.e. economic analysis) and the other evaluated the financial consequences (i.e. financial analysis). Table II also indicates how the various economic consequences were estimated in practice.

Table II Direct and indirect economic effects analysed, diseases covered and methods used to estimate the attributable costs

	Economic effect[a]	Financial effect[a]	Diseases analysed	Estimation method
DIRECT EFFECTS CONSUMPTION				
– Resources devoted to production and distribution	-			Revenue[b]
– Proceeds from excise duty		+		Revenue[b]
– Disbenefits due to addiction				Wtp[c]
MORBIDITY				
– Cost of hospital care	-	-	Major[d]	Attr.fr[e]
– Cost of outpatient care[f]	-	-	All	Hs&msa[g]
– Cost of medicines[h]	-	-	All	Hs&msa[g]
– Sickness benefits		-	Major[d]	Attr.fr[e]
– Disability benefits		-	Major[d]	Attr.fr[e]
MORTALITY				
– Widow's and orphan's pension:	-	Major[d]	Attr.fr[e]	
OTHER DIRECT EFFECTS				
– Fire damage	-	-		Damages[b]
– Cost of health education and research	-	-		Revenue[b]
INDIRECT EFFECTS MORBIDITY				
Lost production due to				
– Sickness absence	-		All	Hs&msa[g]
– Disability	-		Major[d]	Attr.fr[e]
Lost tax-revenues due to				
– Sickness absence		-	All	Hs&msa[g]
– Disability		-	Major[d]	Attr.fr[e]
MORTALITY				
– Lost production	-		Major[d]	Attr.fr[e]
– Avoided health care expenditu		+	Major[d]	Attr.fr[e]
– Lost tax-revenues		-	Major[d]	Attr.fr[e]
– Avoided pension payments		+	Major[d]	Attr.fr[e]
– Other avoided social security benefits		+	Major[d]	Attr.fr[e]

a = cost/expenditure (-), benefit/saving (+), b = statistics, c = willingness to pay estimate, d = cancers of oral cavity, oesophagus, pancreas, larynx, lung and urinary bladder, coronary heart disease, aortic aneurysm, other peripheral vascular diseases, chronic bronchitis and emphysema, e = attributable fraction, f = hospitals, health centres, occupational care and private physician services, g = national health survey and multivariate statistical analysis, h = prescribed and over the counter medicines.

Figure II The relationship between social costs, institutional external costs and final external costs of smoking (Pekurinen, 1991)

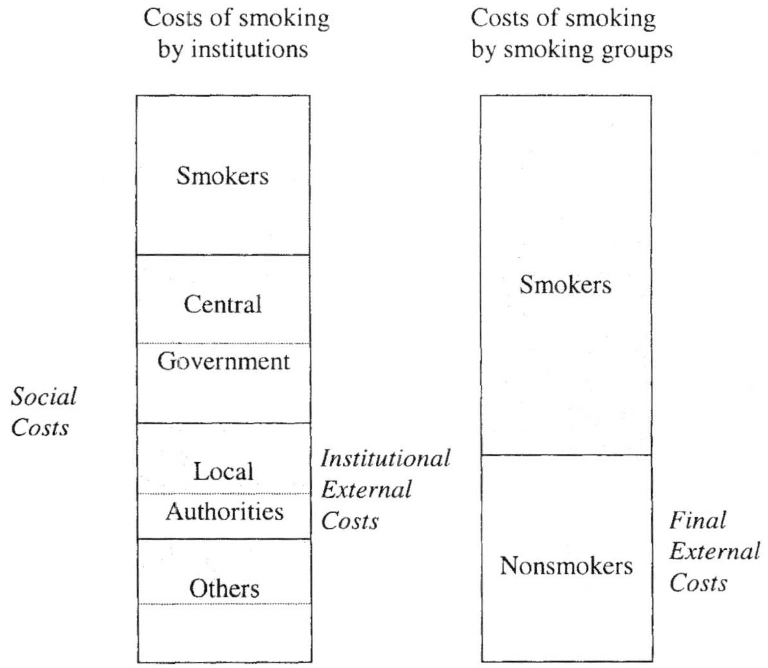

In general, the prevalence approach was used. In some cases, the analysis covered all diseases, but in most cases it focused on the top 24 diseases most commonly documented to be associated with smoking (Doll *et al.*, 1994; Leu and Schaub, 1983).

Attributable fractions were estimated separately for men and women by five-year age groups. Prevalence of smoking in each age- and sex-group used to estimate the attributable fractions was based on the prevalence rates prevailing 10 years before the study year. Disease-specific relative risks were adopted from the most well known epidemiological studies applied in comparable social cost studies. In the 1987 study, we used relative risks from Cederlöf *et al.*, 1975, Doll and Peto, 1976, and Hammond, 1966. In this study on 1995, we used relative risks from Cederlöf *et al.*, 1975, Doll *et al.*, 1994, and Hammond, 1966.

In some cases, attributable fractions were based on a multivariate statistical analysis of a large national health survey (Kalimo *et al.*, 1982). In some cases actual expenditures were used. Disbenefit due to addiction was evaluated in terms of willingness to pay to give up smoking for those who had attempted to stop smoking.

Estimated direct costs and expenditures represent true costs and expenditures someone has to pay in the end. Indirect costs reflect the standard human capital values with appropriate adjustments for age and sex-specific unemployment rates and work-force participation rates.

Indirect expenditures and savings represent tax revenues lost, as well as health expenditures and social security benefits avoided due to early death.

External costs falling on various institutions were estimated by using the respective financing shares of the costs concerned, e.g. the state, local authorities, insurance companies and patients jointly finance hospital costs. Patients financed around 10% of the costs of hospital care in 1995 and other parties financed the rest (Kansaneläkelaitos, 1997). This 10% is the proportion of smoking induced costs that fall directly on smokers and the rest 90% fall on other parties, e.g. local authorities.

External costs falling on nonsmokers were estimated by using individual data from large national health survey and individual tax-register data which were linked together and analysed by smoking groups (Pekurinen, 1991). This allowed us to estimate how smokers and nonsmokers contributed to financing expenditures by the government, local authorities, social security, etc. This in turn enabled us to estimate, for example, the proportion of smoking-related health care expenditures eventually paid by smokers and nonsmokers.

MAIN RESULTS

Main health, resource, cost and financial consequences of smoking in Finland in 1995 and changes between 1987 and 1995 are summarised in Tables III to VII.

Table III indicates that smoking is still a major source of public health problems in Finland, although smoking related illness and premature mortality has come down dramatically from 1987. About 4 090 premature deaths (8.3% of all) of people over 35 years of age were attributed to smoking in 1995. Around 7% of the days of illness due to sickness absence and around 1.4% of the disability pensions were attributed to smoking in 1995.

Smoking-related morbidity, in terms of days of illness, fell over 40% between 1987 and 1995. The number of smoking-related deaths among people aged 35-64 fell by 27%, while the total number of smoking-related deaths for people over 35 years of age fell only by 2% during the same period.

Table III Main health consequences of smoking in Finland in 1995

	Cases in 1995	**(%) of all**	**Change (%) 1987-1995**
Days of illness due to sickness absence	777 000	6.9	-43.9
Individuals on disability pension	3 210	1.4	-40.3
Days of illness due to disability	1 171 000	a	-40.4
Premature deaths (35+ years)	4 090	8.3[b]	-2.1
Premature deaths (35-64 years)	1 155	2.3[c]	-27.6
Life years lost to premature deaths	62 700	a	5.7

a Not estimated.
b 8.6% of all deaths in age group 35 and over.
c 11.9% of all deaths in age group 35-64 years.

Table IV shows that about two average size Finnish acute hospitals and 350 general practitioners were fully occupied year around to treat smoking related illness in Finland in 1995.

Table IV Main resource consequences of smoking in Finland in 1995

	Cases in 1995	**(%) of all**	**Change (%) 1987-1995**
Jobs in tobacco industry	830	a	-32.6
Bed-days in hospitals	240 000	1.6	-11.0
Hospital beds engaged	810	2.1	-10.4
Physician visits	1 052 000	4.1	73.8
General practitioners engaged	350	b	73.8
Working days lost to sickness absence	698 000	6.8	-43.6
Working days lost to disability	706 000	b	-40.2
Working years lost to premature deaths	14 000	b	11.1

a Figure is less than half of the measure.
b Not estimated.

The change in the number of bed-days and physician visits in 1987-1995, shown in Table IV, highlights the dramatic change in treatment patterns of smoking-related and other diseases that has occurred in Finland since the late 1980s. Hospital capacity needed to treat smoking-related cases has fallen by 10%, while the treatment capacity needed in primary care, in terms of physicians, has increased by over 70%.

Table V indicates that the social costs of smoking were estimated to amount to FIM 4,5 billion in 1995, of which about 21% is due to health expenditure and over one third due to lost productivity. The social costs fall short of the minimum estimate of the social benefits of smoking by 18%, as approximated by consumer expenditure on tobacco.

The social costs of smoking have fallen by 28% in real terms in 1987-1995, mainly due to a 47% fall in lost productivity. Smoking-related health expenditure has risen by 26% in 1987-95, mainly due to a 64% increase in outpatient and pharmaceutical expenditure.

Table V Main social costs of smoking in Finland in 1995 (FIM million) and change (%) in 1987-1995 (1995 prices)

	Costs in 1995	**Change (%) 1987-1995**
DIRECT COSTS	2 864	-10.6
– Production & distribution	1 348	-28.4
– Disbenefits due to addiction	566	0.7
– Health expenditure	924	26.0
Inpatient care	*274*	*-18.7*
Outpatient care	*416*	*64.3*
Pharmaceuticals	234	63.7
– Other direct costs	26	10.1
INDIRECT COSTS	1 615	-46.8
– Lost production due to	1 615	-46.8
Sickness absence	*565*	*-50.9*
Disability	*241*	*-58.4*
Premature death	*809*	*-38.1*
TOTAL SOCIAL COSTS	4 479	-28.2

FIM 1 = EURO 0.1682 = CHF 0.28 = $0.18.

Financial consequences of smoking in Finland in 1995 are shown in Table VI. Ignoring tobacco excise, expenditure due to smoking outweighs the financial savings due to it. However, due to tobacco excise smoking appears profitable to the public sector, mainly to the state. For local authorities the net outcome is FIM 270 million negative. In real terms, net revenue due to smoking has remained about the same during the period 1987-1995.

Table VI Main financial consequences of smoking to public sector in Finland in 1995 (FIM million) and change (%) in 1987-1995 (1995 prices)

	Revenue (+)/Expenditure (-) in 1995	**Change (%) 1987-1995**
DIRECT CONSEQUENCES	-973	0.9
– Health expenditure	-697	24.9
– Social security benefits	-260	-34.7
– Other direct expenditure	-16	103.3
INDIRECT CONSEQUENCES	465	-30.4
– Tax revenue lost	-477	-33.3
– Avoided health expenditure	550	-4.7
– Avoided social security benefits	392	-51.4
NET REVENUE (tobacco excise excluded)	-508	71.4
TOBACCO EXCISE	3 110	9.7
NET REVENUE (tobacco excise included)	2 602	2.5

FIM 1 = EURO 0.1682 = CHF 0.28 = $0.18.

External costs of smoking shown in Table VII imply that smokers themselves pay the major part of the social costs of smoking. The estimated institutional external costs amount to 41% of the total social costs. When smokers' contribution to the financing of the institutions concerned is accounted for, smokers pay two thirds of the total social costs. The estimated final external costs are 35% of the total social costs. Revenue from tobacco excise is 1,7-2,0 times higher than the estimated external costs.

Table VII Institutional and final external costs of smoking in Finland in 1995 (FIM million) and change (%) in 1987-1995 (1995 prices)

	External costs 1995		**Change (%) in costs 1987-1995**	
	Institutional	Final	Institutional	Final
DIRECT COSTS	733	571	18.1	-4.2
INDIRECT COSTS	1 090	1 005	-38.7	-25.0
TOTAL	1 823	1 576	-24.0	-18.6
(%) of all social costs	41	35	2.0	2.0
TOBACCO EXCISE	3 110	3 110	9.7	9.7
Tobacco excise/External costs	1.7	2.0		

FIM 1 = EURO 0.1682 = CHF 0.28 = $0.18.

IS THERE A CASE FOR GOVERNMENT INTERVENTION?

The results reported here imply that there may not be a case for government intervention to correct for financial externality of smoking in Finland. The case for intervention may even have weakened substantially between 1987 and 1995.

It seems likely that smokers as a group pay generously for the external costs they generate to others, irrespective of what is assumed about addiction and awareness of the health risks. There may, however, be a case for intervention to correct for market failures other than financial externality.

(i) If consumers are fully informed about the health risks and not addicted to tobacco, government intervention may be justified to correct for caring externality. This requires that the value of the caring externality exceed FIM 375 000 per life lost due to smoking, or FIM 25 000 per life-year lost.

(ii) If consumers are unaware of the health risks, but not addicted to tobacco, there may be a case for government intervention to correct for the lack of information. In this case, the implied value of the caring externality should exceed FIM 130 000 per life lost due to smoking or FIM 9 000 per life-year lost to justify intervention.

(iii) If consumers are unaware of the health risks and addicted to tobacco, there may be a case for government intervention to correct for the lack of information and dependency. This intervention will be justified if caring externality has a positive value.

(iv) If consumers are fully informed about the health risks and addicted to tobacco, there may be a case for government intervention to correct for dependency. If the value of caring externality exceeds FIM 210 000 per life lost due to smoking or FIM 14 000 per life-year lost, government may intervene to prevent addiction and to help smokers to give up smoking.

CONCLUSIONS

The purpose of this study was to analyse the economic consequences of smoking in Finland in 1995 and to compare the results with the original study for 1987.

The investigation of the health and economic consequences of smoking in Finland leads to seven main conclusions:

(1) Smoking appears to be a major source of public health problems, but the magnitude of the problem is declining. Around a third of the estimated decline in smoking-related illness and mortality in 1987-1995 may be due to a drop in smoking prevalence and consumption of tobacco. The rest is due to a change in overall illness and mortality and revised relative risks.

(2) Smoking appears to have a relatively greater impact on public health than on health care resources, but the gap is narrowing. Smoking-related use of hospital care has come down from 1987 to 1995, but slower than smoking-related illness and premature mortality. At the same time, use of primary care physician services has increased substantially.

(3) The social costs of smoking are significant but fall clearly short of the minimum estimate of the social benefits of smoking as approximated by consumers' expenditure on tobacco. The situation has reversed to 1987, mainly because of a substantial drop in the social costs of smoking.

(4) The social costs of smoking have fallen by 28% between 1987 to 1995. Around half of this drop in the social costs may be attributed to a decline in the prevalence of smoking and in the consumption of tobacco.

(5) Financial consequences of smoking-related illness and premature mortality indicate significant net expenditure to the public sector at large, but proceeds from the tobacco excise compensates this generously. It seems evident that smoking is very profitable to the public sector, apart from local authorities.

(6) Smokers themselves pay the major part of the estimated social costs of smoking. It seems likely that smokers as a group pay the external costs they generate to nonsmokers and relevant institutions, irrespective of what is assumed about addiction and awareness of the health risks.

(7) There does not appear to be a case for government intervention to correct for financial externality in Finland. There may be a case for intervention to correct for the caring externality, imperfect information and tobacco addiction.

REFERENCES

Atkinson, A. and Meade, T. (1974), "Methods and Preliminary Findings in Assessing the Economic and Health Service Consequences of Smoking, With Particular Reference to Lung Cancer", *Journal of the Royal Statistical Society*, Series A, Vol. 137, pp. 297-312.

Cederlöf, R., Friberg, L., Hrubec, Z. and Lorich, U. (1975), *The Relationship of Smoking and Some Covariables to Mortality and Cancer Morbidity. A Ten-years Follow-up in a Probability Sample of 55'000 Swedish Subjects Age 18-69,* Karolinska Institutet, Stockholm.

Doll, R. and Peto, R. (1976), "Mortality in Relationship to Smoking: 20 Years' Observations on Male British Doctors", *British Medical Journal*, ii, pp. 1525-1536.

Doll, R., Peto, R., Wheatley, K., Gray, R. and Sutherland, I. (1994), "Mortality in Relationship to Smoking: 40 Years' Observations on Male British Doctors", *British Medical Journal*, Vol. 309, pp. 901-911.

Hammond, E. (1966), "Smoking in Relation to the Deaths of One Million Men and Women", in: Haenszel, W. (Ed.), *Epidemiological Approaches to the Study of Cancer and Other Chronic Diseases*, National Cancer Institute Monograph, No. 19, Washington.

Hodgson, T.A. and Meiners, M.R. (1982), "Cost-of-illness Methodology: A Guide to Current Practices and Procedures", *The Milbank Quarterly*, Vol. 60, pp. 429-462.

Kalimo, E., Nyman, K., Klaukka, T., Tuomikoski, H. and Savolainen, E (1982), *Need, Use and Expenses of Health Services in Finland 1964-1976*, Kansaneläkelaitoksen Julkaisuja A:18, Kansaneläkelaitos, Helsinki, (in Finnish with English summary).

Kansaneläkelaitos (1997), *Health care costs and financing in Finland 1960-95,* Kansaneläkelaitoksen Julkaisuja T9:54, Kansaneläkelaitos, Helsinki, (in Finnish with English summary).

Leu, R.E. and Schaub, T. (1983), "Der Einfluss des Rauchens auf die Mortalität und die Lebenserwartung der Schweizer Wohnbevölkerung", *Schweizerische Medizinische Wochenschrift,* Vol. 113, pp. 3-14.

Markandya, A. and Pearce, P. (1989), "The Social Costs of Tobacco Smoking", *British Journal of Addiction*, Vol. 84, pp. 1139-1150.

Pekurinen, M. (1991), *Economic Aspects of Smoking – Is There a Case for Government Intervention in Finland?* Research Reports 16/1991, National Agency for Welfare and Health, VAPK Publishing, Helsinki.

Rice, D.P., Hodgson, T.A., Sinsheimer, P., Browner, W. and Kopstein, A.N. (1986), "The Economic Costs of the Health Effects of Smoking", *The Milbank Quarterly,* Vol. 64, pp. 489-547.

Statistics Finland (1998), "Tobacco Statistics 1997", *Official Statistics of Finland,* Health 1998:1, Statistics Finland, Helsinki.

8

SOCIAL COST OF SMOKING IN SWITZERLAND

FRANCE PRIEZ
CLAUDE JEANRENAUD
SARINO VITALE
ANDREAS FREI

INTRODUCTION

Smoking is a major concern in public health policy as it produces numerous adverse effects on health. Some of them, such as lung cancer or chronic bronchitis, are mainly attributable to tobacco use, whereas others are related partly to smoking – e.g. mouth cancer or atherosclerosis. The impact of these disorders is usually assessed by means of non-monetary indicators, for example the number of deaths or disabilities related to smoking, the frequency of work incapacity, or the number of potential life years lost as a consequence of smoking. There were 8,300 deaths – or one in six – and more than 16,000 individuals who became disabled due to smoking in 1995 in Switzerland. We estimated that approximately 50,000 years of potential life and more than 5 billion working days were lost. This data reveals the magnitude of the adverse outcomes of smoking, but does not provide a global picture of the burden placed on society. The aim of the present study was to estimate the economic and non-economic consequences of smoking[1]. By using monetary values one can summarise the numerous adverse effects

---

[1] The Swiss Federal Office of Public Health commissioned the present study in order to obtain an up-to-date estimate of the burden smoking represents for the community. Research contract V 8057.

expressed in a single figure: the social cost of tobacco consumption. In Switzerland, a study conducted by Leu and Schaub (1985) valued the economic costs of smoking for 1976.

It is interesting to note that, when assessing costs, the quality of the estimates depends to a large extent on that of the epidemiological data. In particular, it is necessary to obtain reliable information on the number of smoking-related deaths, temporary incapacity days and disability cases[2].

Table I *Epidemiological data on smoking in Switzerland, 1995*

	Deaths	**Years of potential life lost**	**Disability cases**	**Days of temporary incapacity**
Men	6,900	40,300	13,300	3,127,600
Women	1,400	9,400	2,800	2,252,100
Total	**8,300**	**49,700**	**16,100**	**5,379,700**

Sources: Frei (1998) and own estimations.

The definition of social cost and the methodology adopted for its assessment are presented in the following section. The next three sections focus on the estimation of each component of the social cost, that is to say, the direct, indirect and intangible costs. The social cost estimate is discussed in the final section.

METHODOLOGY

Social cost and its components

The social cost of smoking is defined as the monetary value of the economic and non-economic adverse health outcomes of tobacco consumption borne by smokers, their families and relatives, as well as the population at large. Social cost has three components which correspond to three different types of costs. The *direct costs* correspond to the health care costs, that is to say the resources required by medical care – outpatient care, hospital care, physician fees and medication – for all smoking-related diseases. The

[2] In Switzerland, data is available for mortality but there is a lack of information for some aspects of morbidity.

indirect costs capture the value of sacrificed human capital. They represent the loss of production due to short-term incapacity, disability and premature deaths. The marketable production at the workplace as well as the household production losses were estimated. In order to obtain an evaluation of the tangible costs of smoking, we added up direct and indirect costs. Tangible costs represent the sacrifice of resources, whereas a reduction in the frequency of smoking-related illnesses releases resources which then are available for other purposes. The third category of costs – the *intangible costs* – corresponds to the adverse effects of diseases on the quality of life and the life expectancy of smokers and on the quality of life of their relatives due to smokers' sickness or death. Quality of life has an economic value, since individuals are willing to sacrifice a part of their income to improve it. It should be noted that some elements of costs essentially attributable to smoking habits – such as the reduction in productivity at work or the consequences of passive smoking – were not taken in consideration in the present study.

The social cost of smoking can be determined for all patients suffering from smoking-related diseases during a specific year – the so-called prevalence-based approach – or only for new cases diagnosed during the reference year using an incidence-based approach. We estimated the direct and indirect costs in a prevalence-based framework and the intangible costs by means of a lifetime or incidence-based approach.

The "extended COI" approach

Most studies of the social cost of addictive behaviours are based on the traditional "cost-of-illness" approach (COI) which permits the valuation of the economic burden of diseases and premature deaths (Rice *et al.*, 1986; Single *et al.*, 1996). The direct costs are usually estimated by the replacement costs method, and the indirect costs are assessed by calculating the value of forgone income using the human capital approach. COI estimates do not reflect the true cost of smoking, because they do not include the intangible costs. Thus, COI results should be considered as a partial estimation of the social cost of smoking. Another measure of the cost of smoking-related diseases is given by the amount people are willing to pay to reduce the risk of disease. The "willingness-to-pay" approach (WTP) offers the advantage of capturing intangible as well as part of the tangible costs. This approach is applied increasingly in health economics because it makes it possible to assess the quality of life as well as the economic consequences of disease or treatment (Diener, 1998). In the present study, we adopted a new approach – called extended cost-of-illness – that combines the WTP approach with the replacement costs and the human capital methods. With this procedure each component of the social cost can be valued separately. The human capital and the replacement costs approaches were applied to assess the tangible costs. The intangible costs were valued by the contingent valuation (CV) method. The CV survey was designed carefully in order to value only the intangible component of the social cost. To avoid double-counting, we used the net approach when assessing indirect mortality costs. If smokers did not die prematurely, they would contribute to the general welfare with their production, but they would also consume. Thus, in order to obtain net indirect costs, the individuals' expected lifetime consumption is subtracted from the expected lifetime production (Pekurinen, 1991).

Figure I Methods of estimation

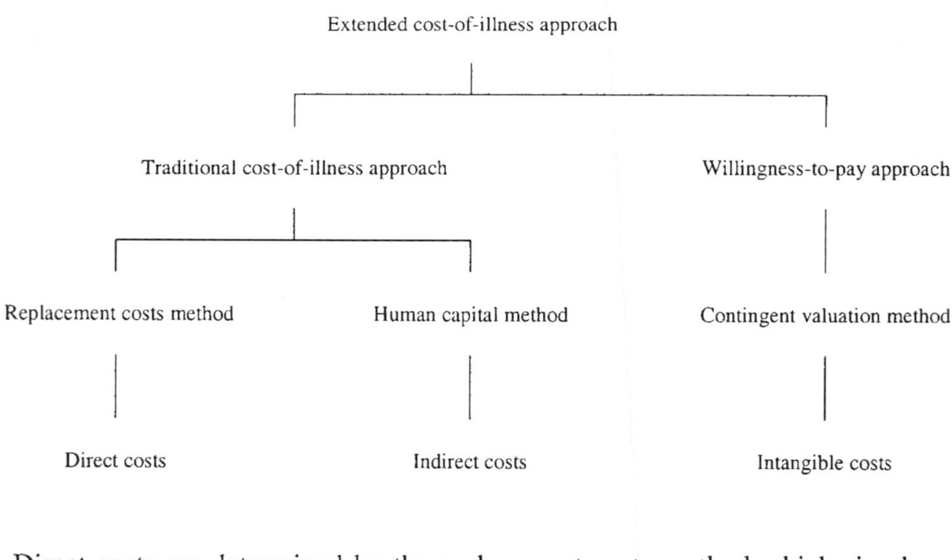

Direct costs are determined by the replacement costs method which simply values the resources employed to prevent or mitigate the consequences of smoking on health. We considered the gross health care costs, i.e. we did not value the potential reduction in health care expenditure arising from smoking-related premature death. Some economists argue that the longer life expectancy of non-smokers generates direct costs in their extra years of life which may compensate for the treatment costs of smoking-related diseases (Warner, 1998; Barendregt *et al.*, 1997).

The human capital (HC) method provides an estimate of individuals' potential output. Indirect costs correspond to the value of production lost as a consequence of smoking-related morbidity and mortality. Short-term and long-term work incapacity due to disease or disability reduces the nation output. When temporarily ill or disabled, individuals do not take part in the production process and have difficulties performing household chores. The consequences of premature deaths are assessed considering the value of the production expected until the workers' retirement age. According to the advocates of the friction method, the main drawback of the HC approach lies in the assumption that firms cannot replace the ill or deceased employees by hiring unemployed individuals (see Koopmanschap in this volume). In fact, in Switzerland employers would be unable to find individuals to replace the incapacitated workers as the labour market is tight – according to the OECD, unemployment in Switzerland is mainly structural.

Based on welfare economics, the WTP approach relies on individual preferences in order to attribute a price to non-tradable goods. It values health either by considering the choice made by individuals in an actual market – the so-called revealed preferences – or by asking people what they would be willing to pay to reduce the probability of morbidity or mortality – the expressed preferences. The contingent valuation (CV) method is in the latter category and is commonly used to estimate the value of risk variation. A hypothetical market – the contingent market – is presented to interviewees in order to incite them to express their WTP to reduce their risk of illness or death. With this approach one can assess the impact of smoking-related diseases on quality of life. Most of the CV studies include tangible and intangible consequences of health disorders. Nevertheless, with an appropriate design of the questionnaire, it is possible to exclude the economic effects and to value the intangible costs only.

DIRECT COSTS

The replacement costs method was applied to value resources devoted to outpatient treatment, short- and long-term hospitalisation. Outpatient care includes visits to doctors and medication. Treatment in hospital outpatients services is included in hospital costs. These smoking-related health care costs were estimated for 15 diagnostic groups according to the ICD-9 coding scheme (Appendix). The public policy costs – prevention, research and training –, the value of property losses caused by fires associated with smoking and the administrative costs are not included in the estimated cost. In accordance with the international guidelines for COI studies, we did not include in the social cost the value of the resources used to produce cigarettes (U.S. DHHS, 1992; Single in this volume). It should be noted that the satisfaction tobacco products give to consumers was not included either.

In 1995, the estimated direct costs amounted to CHF 1.2 billion (Table II) or CHF 171.6 per capita. Hospital costs accounted for three fourths of these costs with CHF 917 million. Considered by gender, men generated two thirds of direct costs with CHF 808.0 million. The prevalence of smoking-related diseases is significantly higher for men.

Table II Direct costs of smoking in CHF mio, 1995

	Outpatient care		Hospital care		Total
	Doctors' fees	**Medication**	**Short-stays**	**Long-stays**	
Men	110.0	52.0	632.0	14.0	808.0
Women	90.0	42.0	244.0	27.0	404.0
Total	**200.0**	**94.0**	**876.0**	**41.0**	**1,212.0**

Source: Frei (1998).

The direct costs of smoking accounted for 0.3% of the Swiss GDP. This result is similar to the value obtained by Single *et al.* (1996) for Canada (0.4%) and by Pekurinen (1991) for Finland (0.3%).

INDIRECT COSTS

The loss of production caused by premature death, short-term work incapacity and disability was estimated for fifteen smoking-related diagnostic groups using the human capital methodology. The forgone production at the workplace as well as the value of the household production of the deceased were measured. The reduction in household work is the consequence of the inability to perform household chores and to attend to the education of one's children. We applied the opportunity cost method to assess this non-marketable production. It postulates that the value of household work corresponds to the income the ill or disabled individual would have earned if she or he had devoted the same amount of time to her or his professional activity.

Not all indirect costs of smoking were measured: the reduction in productivity at work due to smoking habits and the impact of mortality and morbidity on charity and volunteer work were disregarded for lack of data.

Indirect costs of mortality

In 1995, 3,487 men and 737 women died because of smoking, between ages 35 and 74. The Swiss Labour Force Survey shows that a significant part of the population – 8% of women and 15% of men – still held gainful employment after the legal age of retirement – 62 for women and 65 for men. After the age of 74 the marketable production is considered to be sufficiently low to be ignored (OFS, 1995).

Indirect mortality costs were obtained by discounting the future expected gross earnings of the deceased by gender and age. The survival probability, the labour market participation rate and the average occupation rate for women and men at various ages, as well as the probability of being unemployed were taken into account. As household production losses were estimated by the opportunity cost method, they were valued by considering the gross annual income, the survival probability and the mean time devoted to household chores according to gender and age.

The productivity of the marketable and household production is expected to grow at a rate of 1% p.a. A sensitivity analysis was conducted by applying three different discount rates: 0%, 2% and 6%[3]. The results illustrated in Table III are based on a 2% discount rate which corresponds to the actual interest rate of Government bonds.

The gross indirect costs of mortality amounted to CHF 1.8 billion and almost half this amount – CHF 826.9 million – corresponds to losses in household services. Net production losses of CHF 1.2 billion were obtained by subtracting the value of the discounted lifetime consumption of the prematurely deceased. It is not surprising that the breakdown by gender reveals that 80% of the net indirect costs were generated by men. As in the case of direct costs, there is a direct relation between this proportion of indirect costs and the significant difference in the occurrence of smoking-related deaths among men and women.

---

[3] 6% is an estimate of the marginal rate of return for private investment in Switzerland in 1995. Some authors (Barendregt *et al.*, 1997) consider that a zero discount rate has some justifications for valuing health outcomes. See Viscusi (1995) for a different point of view.

Indirect costs of morbidity

Due to the lack of reliable data about tobacco-related morbidity, the frequency of short-term work incapacity and disability were estimated using German data (Frei, 1998). In 1995, smoking-related diseases caused more than 300,000 short-term absences from work resulting in a loss of more than 4 million working days. The number of individuals who became disabled as a result of smoking exceeded 16,000 (Table I).

The indirect costs of morbidity were estimated at CHF 2.6 billion, short-term incapacity representing a loss of CHF 1.6 billion and disability a sacrifice in production of 1 billion. On the whole, household production losses accounted for about 30% of the indirect costs of morbidity.

Total indirect costs

Table III Indirect costs of smoking, in CHF mio, 1995

Production losses	Men	Women	Total
Mortality*			
Marketable	913.3	88.8	1,002.1
Household	556.0	270.9	826.9
Gross total	1,469.3	359.7	1,829.0
Expected consumption	*-486.3*	*-120.3*	*-606.6*
Net total	**983.0**	**239.4**	**1,222.4**
Temporary incapacity			
Marketable	830.2	234.2	1,064.4
Household	222.5	281.6	504.1
Total	**1,052.7**	**515.8**	**1,568.5**
Disability			
Marketable	688.7	58.9	747.6
Household	191.5	79.5	271.0
Total	**880.2**	**138.4**	**1,018.6**
Total net indirect costs	**2,915.9**	**893.6**	**3,809.5**

* 2% discount rate.

The total net indirect costs attributable to smoking-related mortality and morbidity represented a loss of CHF 3.8 billion or CHF 538 per capita. In terms of GDP – 1% –, it is comparable with the proportion obtained in other studies. Collins *et al.* (1991) estimated it at 0.6% of the Australian GDP. The result for Canada amounted to 1% of GDP, but the study valued gross indirect costs (Single *et al.*, 1996). Unlike the present study, the Canadian and Australian studies did not value household production losses.

INTANGIBLE COSTS

The human capital approach ignores the intrinsic value of quality of life and thus strongly underestimates the social cost of illness. It has also been criticised for placing a high value on young and well-educated people and a very low one on the health of the elderly and of those who are not in the labour force. Furthermore, it assigns no value to intangible outcomes such as pain, suffering and reduced life expectancy. The health consequences of smoking reduce the quality of life of patients as it generates physical and mental pain due to the disorder itself and to its treatment. Life style, social life as well as the relations within the family are altered and the reduction in life expectancy causes psychological consequences for ill or disabled individuals. The quality of life of relatives is reduced because of the distress they face with the patients' sickness, and because of the grief and suffering due to the smoker's premature death. It should be noted that other intangible consequences of smoking, such as the physical discomfort of the smokers, the cost of the addiction and the consequences of passive smoking for relatives and the community were not assessed.

The intangible costs of six smoking-related illnesses were valued: two respiratory disorders – lung cancer and chronic bronchitis – and four cardiovascular diseases – angina pectoris, stroke, fatal and non-fatal heart attack. They were selected according to two criteria: the smoking attributable fraction and the incidence of the disease[4].

For lung cancer, chronic bronchitis and fatal heart attack, the assessment of the intangible costs was based on a direct risk-against-money trade-off. Interviewees were asked to state their WTP to lower the risk of contracting

---

[4] Attributable fractions range from 0.39 for angina pectoris to 0.88 for lung cancer. More than 2,000 cases were diagnosed in 1995 for each of the six selected diseases (Frei, 1998).

the disease. For angina pectoris, stroke and non-fatal heart attack, the loss of quality of life was valued using a two-step procedure: in the first step, each state of health was assessed in utility terms on a rating scale. In the second step, intangible costs were derived from comparing the valuation on the rating scale with the monetary estimates of the other three diseases.

Methodology

The CV questionnaire was designed carefully in order to avoid potential biases (Arrow *et al.*, 1993). Two focus groups were set up and a pre-test was conducted to improve the design of the contingent market and of the questionnaire.

The risk reduction offered in the contingent market may be of benefit to society or only to those who pay for it (Bala *et al.*, 1999). In the first case, health is a public good, as people surveyed reveal their WTP to improve public health, for example, by financing a prevention campaign. In the second case, respondents consider their personal risk and each stated WTP corresponds to the value each respondent attributes to her or his own quality of life. In this study, we designed the contingent market in order to value health as a private good.

Individuals in the surveyed population may be patients with the disease – ex post approach – or the population at risk – ex ante approach (Dolan, 1998). For patients suffering from a life-threatening disease such as lung cancer or heart attack, the risk-money trade-off would be unrealistic. Interviewees would probably be willing to sacrifice more than their income to recover full health because health has no substitute. Another source of concern is that people with a given disease might behave in a strategic way and state amounts exceeding their loss of quality of life. For all these reasons we adopted the ex ante approach: the target population includes all individuals 18 years old and above.

The assessed good – a reduction in the risk of contracting a specific smoking-related disease – must be described precisely. To do so, the interviewees were given three different types of information: a precise, but short, summary of the health implications of the disorder[5], the general population's average risk of contracting it and the main risk factors of the

---

[5] Dr. Marco Vannotti, from the Outpatients Medical Clinic at the University of Lausanne, helped us in the description of tne health implications of the six selected smoking-related diseases.

disease. This information allowed respondents to estimate their own personal risk. Then, they were asked to express their WTP to benefit from a vaccine. It was specified that the inoculation would be effective during one year and would reduce their own risk of contracting the disease by 95%.

In May 1998, 868 personal interviews were conducted in the three main linguistic regions of Switzerland. We used the quota sampling technique, and the following criteria were applied to select the surveyed population: area of residence – rural or urban –, age, gender and social stratum.

Results

To assess the internal validity of the CV survey, we used a semi-logarithmic and a Box-Cox model[6]. The dependant variable is the marginal willingness-to-pay (MWTP) which is defined as the price respondents agree to pay for a risk reduction of 1 in 100,000.

For lung cancer, chronic bronchitis and fatal heart attack, the estimated Box-Cox model is comparable with the semi-logarithmic one, as the Box-Cox parameter is close to zero in each of the three models[7]. Thus, we used the semi-logarithmic model to estimate the mean and median MWTP. The intangible costs per case are obtained by multiplying the estimated mean MWTP by 100,000[8]. The intangible costs of angina pectoris, stroke and non-fatal heart attack were valued indirectly based on the relative weights of the six diseases on the rating scale.

---

[6] The semi-logarithmic and the Box-Cox models reduce the influence of outliers – very high bids expressed by some respondents – and thus partly correct the hypothetical bias (McClelland *et al.*, 1991).

[7] If the value of the Box-Cox parameter (λ) is zero, the functional form is the semi-logarithmic one and if $\lambda = 1$, the Box-Cox specification corresponds to the linear model. In the present study, the λ value is 0.11 for lung cancer, 0.12 for chronic bronchitis and 0.15 for fatal heart attack. Thus, the best fit was fairly close to the semi-logarithmic model.

[8] The mean MWTP appeared to be a better estimator of intangible costs than the median. The MWTP distribution is strongly bimodal, probably because many non-smokers knew they were at low risk and were not willing to pay for the vaccine. It is interesting to note that positive MWTP has a normal distribution. Thus, from an economic point of view, the median would seriously underestimate MWTP.

Table IV Intangible costs of smoking, 1995

	MWTP in CHF	Intangible costs	
		Per case in CHF thousands	Total in CHF mio
Lung cancer	5.125	512.5	1,305.3
Chronic bronchitis	0.385	38.5	386.3
Fatal heart attack	2.360	236.0	593.5
Angina pectoris	2.001	200.1	831.0
Stroke	2.414	241.4	976.7
Non-fatal heart attack	2.181	218.1	868.3
Total intangible costs			**4,961.1**

Respondents considered lung cancer as generating the most serious consequences for quality of life, with intangible costs exceeding CHF 500,000 per case (Table IV). This was twice the value attributed to fatal heart attack. This means that people place a lower price on sudden death than on a severe chronic disease, such as lung cancer. According to interviewees, the less serious disorder is chronic bronchitis with intangible costs of CHF 38,500. This indicates that individuals place a much lower value on a chronic disease which is not perceived as life-threatening.

The total intangible costs of the six selected smoking-related diseases amounted to about CHF 5 billion or 1.3% of the Swiss GDP. Lung cancer generates the largest share with CHF 1.3 billion, and chronic bronchitis accounts for the smallest share with CHF 386.3 million. In other studies, reduced quality of life and premature death have rarely been included in the estimates of the social cost of smoking. Collins *et al.* (1991) used the value of the expected lifetime consumption of the deceased and made a conservative estimate of the loss of life, based on the literature, as a proxy for intangible costs.

CONCLUSION

The social cost of smoking-related adverse health effects is the addition of direct, net indirect and intangible costs. The question of how the indirect costs of mortality are to be determined gives rise to lengthy debate. Should gross production losses or the forgone production less the reduction in consumption resulting from the premature death of smokers be considered? If we consider net forgone production, indirect mortality costs represent the present value of the production which is lost to society. According to our definition of tangible and intangible costs, we had to choose net production losses when adding up the various components of social cost (Vitale *et al.*, 1998; Collins *et al.*, 1991). In fact, the value of the expected lifetime consumption can be viewed as a minimum estimate of individuals' well-being which is already included in intangible costs. The second precaution which was taken to avoid double-counting, was to design the questionnaire in such a way that interviewees would only consider the consequences of the disease for their quality of life. During CV interviews, each respondent was told that the disease would alter her or his quality of life, without any adverse financial impact. A debriefing question helped to check whether respondents had valued intangible effects only when stating their WTP.

Figure II Social cost of smoking in Switzerland in CHF mio, 1995

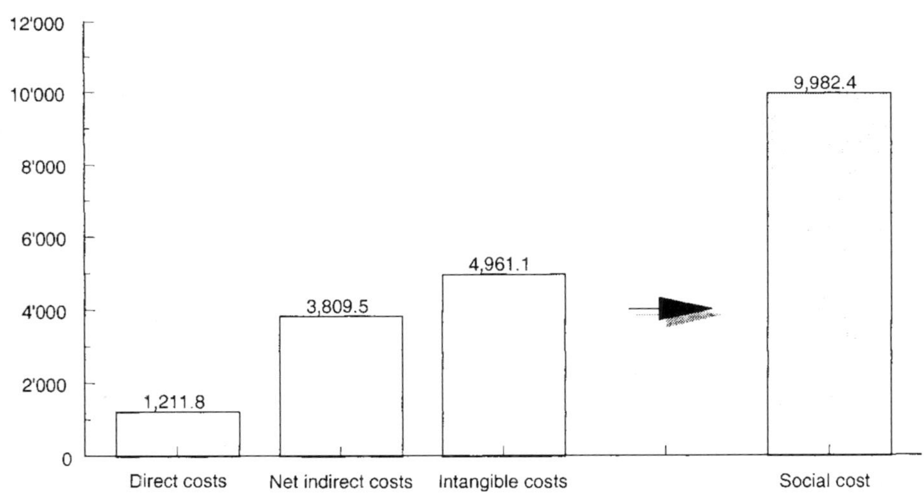

In 1995, the social cost of smoking was estimated at CHF 10 billion or CHF 1,416 per capita (Figure II). It accounts for 2.7% of the Swiss GDP, which is slightly higher than in other empirical studies. Single *et al.* (1995) obtained 1.4% of the Canadian GDP and Rice *et al.* (1986) 2.0% of the U.S. GDP. These lower values are mainly due to the fact that these studies assessed tangible costs only. In the Australian study by Collins *et al.* (1991), which entails a conservative estimate of intangible costs, the social cost accounted for 2.4% of GDP, which is closer to the figure we obtained for Switzerland.

On the whole, the present estimation of the social cost of smoking may be considered as conservative. The direct and indirect costs of morbidity and mortality were based on the fifteen main smoking-related diagnostic groups. Nevertheless, the relative risk for smokers and former smokers exceeds 1 in a broader set of diseases (Abelin, 1992; U.S. DHHS, 1992)[9]. Moreover, intangible costs were estimated for six diagnostic groups only. When estimating the indirect costs of morbidity, work incapacity up to the legal retirement age only was considered, even if household production losses may be significant after that age. The consequences of passive smoking were not included in the estimation of intangible costs, despite their impact on the quality of life of the smokers' relatives and that of the general population.

This study benefited from the extensive research studies which have assessed the disability, morbidity and mortality attributable to smoking since the first attempt was made to value the cost of smoking in Switzerland (Leu *et al.*, 1985). We also took advantage of the improvement in valuation methods used to assess one component of social cost which has rarely been taken into account: the loss of quality of life. Thus, the present estimation includes the tangible and intangible consequences of smoking and it provides a broad estimation of the adverse outcomes of this addictive behaviour for the community.

---

[9] The relative risk of smoking is defined as the incidence of the disease among smokers or former smokers divided by the incidence of this disease among non-smokers.

REFERENCES

Abelin T. (1992), "En 1990, plus de 10'000 décès dus au tabagisme en Suisse", *Bulletin de l'Office fédéral de la santé publique*, N° 8, pp. 101-105.

Arrow K., Solow R., Portney P.R., Leamer E.E., Radner R. and Schuman H. (1993), "Report of the NOAA Panel on Contingent Valuation", *Federal Register*, N° 52, pp. 4601-4614.

Bala M.V., Mauskopf J.A. and Wood L.L. (1999), "Willingness to Pay as a Measure of Health Benefits", *PharmacoEconomics*, vol. 15 (1), pp. 9-18.

Barendregt J.J., Bonneux L. and van der Maas P.J. (1997), "The health care costs of smoking", *New England Journal of Medicine*, Vol. 337, pp. 1052-1057.

Collins D. and Lapsley H. (1991), *Estimating the Economic Costs of Drug Abuse in Australia*, Monograph Series N° 15, Commonwealth Government Printer, Canberra.

Diener A., O'Brien B. and Gafni A. (1998), "Health care contingent valuation studies: a review and classification of the literature", *Health Economics*, N° 7, pp. 313-326.

Dolan P. (1998), "Valuing Health-Related Quality of Life", *PharmacoEconomics*, Vol. 15 (2), pp. 119-127.

Frei A. (1998), *Kostenanalyse des Tabakkonsums in der Schweiz. Teil 1 Epidemiologie, Teil 2 Direkte Kosten*, Rohbericht im Auftrag des Bundesamt für Gesundheit, 23. Juni, Basel.

Leu R.E. and Schaub T. (1985), *Rauchen und Gesundheit. Eine volkswirtschaftliche Analyse*, Institut für Sozialwissenschaften, Universität Basel.

McClelland G.H., Schulze W.D., Waldman D., Irwin J. and Schenk D. (1991), "Sources of Error in Contingent Valuation", in *Valuing the Benefits of Groundwater Cleanup: Interim Report*, Office for Policy Planning and Evaluation, U.S. Environmental Protection Agency, Washington D.C.

Office fédéral de la statistique (1995), *Enquête sur la population active (ESPA). Résultats commentés et tableaux 1994*, OFS, Berne.

Pekurinen M. (1991), *Economic Aspects of Smoking. Is there a case for government intervention in Finland?*, Research Reports 16/1991, National Agency for Welfare and Health, Helsinki.

Rice D.P. and Hodgson T.A. (1986), "The economic costs of the health effects of smoking, 1984", *The Milbank Quarterly*, Vol. 64, N° 4, pp. 489-547.

Single E. Robson L., Xie X. and Rehm J. (1996), *The Costs of Substance Abuse in Canada, highlights of a major study of the health, social and economic costs associated with the use of alcohol, tobacco and illicit drugs*, Canadian Centre on Substance Abuse, Toronto.

U.S. Department of Health and Human Services (1992), *Smoking and Health in the Americas: a 1992 Report of the Surgeon General, in collaboration with the Pan American Health Organization*, DHHS publication N° (CDC) 92-8419.

Viscusi W.K. (1995), "Discounting health effects for medical decisions", in Sloan F.A. (Ed.), *Valuing health care: costs, benefits, and effectiveness of pharmaceuticals and other medical technologies*, Cambridge University Press, Cambridge.

Vitale S., Priez F. and Jeanrenaud C. (1998), *Le coût social de la consommation de tabac en Suisse*, rapport final, Institut de recherches économiques et régionales, Neuchâtel.

Warner K. (1998), "The Economics of Tobacco and Health: an Overview", in Abedian I. and van der Merwe R. (Eds.), *The Economics of Tobacco Control: Towards an optimal policy mix*, Applied Fiscal Research Centre, University of Cape Town.

APPENDIX

Diagnosis related to smoking according to the ICD-9 coding scheme

Diagnosis	ICD-9	Diagnosis	ICD-9
Mouth cancer	140-149	Angina pectoris, ischemic heart diseases	413-414
Esophageal cancer	150	Other forms of heart diseases	420-429
Pancreatic cancer	157	Cerebrovascular diseases	434-436
Laryngeal cancer	161	Atherosclerosis	440-441
Lung cancer	162	Pneumonia	480-486
Bladder cancer	188	Bronchitis and emphysema	490-492
Kidney cancer	189	Asthma	493
Myocardial infarction	410-412		

9

COMMENTARY ON THE SOCIAL COST OF SMOKING IN SWITZERLAND

SANDRA NOCERA

The study on the social costs of smoking in Switzerland conducted by the IRER of the University of Neuchâtel on behalf of the Federal Office of Health reaches conclusions which are corroborated by other studies. The social costs of smoking are high, though the major share of the costs is borne by the smokers themselves.

It is extremely costly to measure all the costs of a human activity such as smoking. The most difficult part is measuring the indirect and intangible costs, which is why they are often simply left out. The authors of the study do, however, attempt to include as much as possible all the cost elements and demonstrate where and how their calculations differ greatly from the selected method and the underlying assumptions. Furthermore, they apply more recent methods, at least by Swiss standards, for example by measuring the intangible costs of smoking on the basis of a survey. In the following commentary, rather than discussing the selected assumptions and models, and their impact on the results in greater depth (since the authors themselves do so clearly), I will highlight the study's possible conclusions from the economic point of view.

The authors attribute great importance to the magnitude of the social cost amounting to CHF 10 billion, which would appear to justify state intervention. From the economic point of view, however, the need for state intervention cannot be concluded merely from the magnitude of the social costs. Such intervention comes naturally when the market fails. In the case of smoking there are three possible causes of market failure: negative external effects, incorrect risk perception and addictive behaviour.

Negative external effects are those costs which are not borne by the "perpetrator" but which are passed on to society. According to the study, health expenditure accounts for the largest share of the external costs of smoking. In this context, the magnitude of external costs depends on the type of prevailing social security system. In Switzerland, health insurance premiums pegged to risk are prohibited, in order to ensure solidarity between the sick and the healthy. In relation to smoking this means that part of health expenditure arising from the higher risk of morbidity is borne by that nonsmokers. It is precisely this solidarity which is considered irritating in the case of smoking; at the same time, the fact that other types of behaviour (e.g. nutrition, physical exercise) also have a massive influence on health risks is disregarded.

Since the life expectancy of smokers is lower, society gets the benefit of savings, not only the brunt of costs. For this reason, the overall negative, external effects of smoking are small and sufficiently internalised by the tobacco tax. The authors pass over the fact, however, that the well-being of nonsmokers, which is impaired by smoke, also accounts for a share of the external costs. This in turn could have been ascertained by means of a survey. Given the generalised ban on smoking nowadays, in the workplace as well as in public buildings, one can assume that this factor is weak and would in no way alter the results of the study.

A second possible cause of market failure can be found in incorrect risk perception. For an individual to be able to act rationally, he or she must have full knowledge of all the consequences of his or her actions. A smoker, who is not informed of the health risk he or she incurs by smoking, takes the decision to smoke unaware of all the consequences, and hence smokes too much. This would justify state intervention, by means of information campaigns about the risk of smoking or by introducing, respectively increasing, the tobacco tax, which could serve as a warning about risk as well as help internalise external costs. Over the last twenty years, intensive information campaigns have been conducted in Switzerland on the risks of smoking, and the tobacco tax exceeds the amount that would be required to internalise the external effects; it would thus appear that incorrect risk perception is not one of the possible causes.

A third cause of market failure is addictive behaviour which could hinder individuals from taking rational decisions. The rational decision to smoke is linked very closely to risk perception. When an individual starts to smoke, fully realising the risks of addiction, the decision is taken perfectly rationally (rational addiction). As discussed above, one can assume that the Swiss population is informed about the risks of smoking and the related risk of addiction, so it is reasonable to exclude the third cause of market failure as well.

There seem to be few economic arguments in favour of additional state intervention with regard to smoking. The social costs are more than covered by the smokers themselves and nowadays the population is supposedly informed about the risks of smoking and the related risk of addiction. There remains the need for permanent information to be provided to the younger generations by making for example information about addiction part of the school curricula.

RISK PERCEPTION, DEMAND AND TAXATION

10

PUBLIC PERCEPTION OF SMOKING RISKS

W. KIP VISCUSI

INTRODUCTION

Cigarette smoking is perhaps the largest single consumer risk that individuals incur on a mass scale. Scientific estimates of the hazards of smoking dwarf the risks associated with motor-vehicle travel, hazardous jobs, and other risky activities. A policy question of fundamental importance is whether people in fact understand these risks and act upon them in a reasonable manner. The point of view that I will take here is that in assessing any market failure, the appropriate reference point is the same as economists apply in other contexts, which is to assess whether people are making informed and rational choices. My primary focus will be on people's assessment of the health risks of smoking[1].

Suppose, for example, that people did not understand the health implications of their smoking decisions. Such a finding would be pertinent to assessing the private cost to the individual. The gap between the expected costs and those that will actually occur based on the true probabilities serves as a measure of the private loss. In addition, to the extent that people are not knowledgeable of the risks, these unanticipated private costs also might be pertinent for various tallies of the social costs of smoking. The principal economic rationale for excluding these private costs is that they are

[1] For a more comprehensive perspective on this literature, see Viscusi (1990, 1991, 1992, 1995, 1998).

anticipated by smokers and hence fully internalised, but if this is not the case then the social calculus must be altered as well.

From a policy standpoint, knowledge of the extent to which people understand the risks associated with smoking should be of fundamental concern. In the United States, for over three decades the government has undertaken mandatory on-product warnings regarding the hazards of smoking, mandatory warnings in advertising, restrictions of advertising, and various public health reports disseminating smoking risk information. These official information sources have obviously been coupled with private information as well, such as that in the media. What has been the outcome of this public information campaign? Do people in fact understand the risks of smoking as one would expect if these public information efforts have been effective? Are there any glaring informational gaps that need to be addressed through further information dissemination efforts? Somewhat surprisingly, this type of question has never been addressed by the public health establishment in the United States. Rather, the focus has been on using the campaigns as a form of persuasion rather that attempting to identify specific information gaps that need to be remedied.

Setting the standard for what consumers should know to be adequately informed can be cast within the context of economists' standard expected utility calculations. For all the various health outcomes associated with smoking, do consumers have a sufficient understanding of the risks? Are they deterred from smoking to the same extent as they would be if they accurately assessed all the pertinent probabilities of the adverse health outcomes linked to smoking? If, for example, consumers were to underestimate the risk of heart disease, this effect could be offset by overestimating the risk of lung cancer. Similarly, consumers may not know the precise chemical constituents of cigarettes, which additives cause cancer and which do not, or similar highly detailed scientific aspects of the risks. Yet, they may nevertheless be knowledgeable in the sense of having risk beliefs that deter smoking to the same extent as would sound processing of the scientific information pertaining to smoking. This paper will attempt to provide a comprehensive perspective on public perception of smoking risks, focusing on the hazards of lung cancer, overall mortality risk, and life expectancy loss.

I shall first discuss the background context of the smoking information that has been disseminated to consumers in the United States. In the following section, I focus on whether this and other information provided to consumers has been sufficient to lead to a perception of the lung cancer risks of smoking, which was the hazard first highlighted by the government in its landmark 1964 report on smoking[2]. This evidence, which is from surveys undertaken in 1985 and 1991, indicates that smokers greatly overestimate the risks of lung cancer. The extent of this risk overestimation is, however, less in the case of mortality risks, which is the focus of the next section. A related issue is the extent of life that people lose through smoking, not simply their probability of death. Estimates for life expectancy loss reported in the penultimate section indicate these hazards are overestimated as well.

SMOKING RISK INFORMATION

Smoking critics often assume that they alone have access to information about the hazards of smoking. For some inexplicable reason, smokers are assumed to either not have had access to this information or have not been able to understand it and have thus been excluded from knowledge of the substantial risks of smoking. This mindset in turn can potentially influence the direction of government policies, leading to greater reliance on hazard warnings when in fact other policy interventions may be more beneficial.

A useful starting point for investigating the basis of the public's knowledge about smoking risks is to consider the information disseminated by the federal government. The 1964 report on the lung cancer risks associated with smoking marked the beginning, not the end, of the public pronouncements on cigarette hazards. Beginning in 1967 the U.S. government issued annual reports on the health consequences of smoking, where these reports were from the U.S. Surgeon General. These reports began more as literature surveys of a general nature, and then evolved into reports with specific themes, such as cancer, nicotine addiction, and cardiovascular disease. None of these reports feature an assessed probability of particular health outcomes. Rather, the emphasis is on the total number of smokers who will incur particular ailments, e.g. 400,000 smokers will die every year because of their smoking activity. Thus, the government has highlighted the numerator of the risk, but not the denominator or the entire calculation that makes clear the probability of the different health effects. One would expect this informational approach to lead to an overestimation of the risk to the extent that highlighting the total number of deaths and other adverse effects creates concern with smoking hazards that is disproportionate to the underlying probabilities. Although the Surgeon

[2] See the U.S. Department of Health Education and Welfare (1964).

General's reports are not widely read by the public, the annual press releases from these reports do receive substantial national publicity.

The warnings themselves for smoking hazards have been mandated by acts of the U.S. Congress. Table I gives the evolution of the three eras of cigarette warnings that have been in place. The initial warning beginning in 1965 indicated that "Cigarette Smoking May Be Hazardous to Your Health." The 1969 warning decreased the probabilistic emphasis, indicating that "The Surgeon General Has Determined That Cigarette Smoking Is Dangerous to Your Health." Thereafter, the warning approach led to a series of four rotating warnings concerning a variety of risks associated with smoking. The advantage of rotating warnings is that more diverse information can be conveyed without cluttering a label, while the disadvantage is that any particular warning will receive less exposure. By law cigarette companies were required to include the boxed warning information in all print ads. Radio and television ads for cigarettes were banned.

Although the warnings do not include any specific quantitative information indicating the level of the risk, a qualitative approach is not unusual in the hazard warnings field. People generally find it easier to process verbal information than a detailed list of statistics pertaining to the risk. Perhaps the most sophisticated group receiving warnings is that of physicians, all of whom have taken courses in pharmacology and related subjects as part of their medical training. However, even the warnings for prescription drugs that are compiled in the *Physicians Desk Reference* often do not include quantitative information pertaining to the level of the hazard posed by the drug. While it is doubtful that all current hazard warnings could be replaced by a quantitative approach, providing some limited quantitative information may nevertheless foster more accurate risk assessments.

Table I Cigarette Warning Content Summaries[a]

Warning period	Warning content
Cigarette warning, 1965	"Caution: Cigarette Smoking May Be Hazardous to Your Health."
Cigarette warning, 1969	"Warning: The Surgeon General Has Determined That Cigarette Smoking Is Dangerous to Your Health."
Cigarette warning, 1984	1. "SURGEON GENERAL'S WARNING: Smoking Causes Lung Cancer, Heart Disease, Emphysema, and May Complicate Pregnancy."
	2. "SURGEON GENERAL'S WARNING: Quitting Smoking Now Greatly Reduces Serious Risks To Your Health."
	3. "SURGEON GENERAL'S WARNING: Smoking by Pregnant Women May Result in Fetal Injury, Premature Birth, and Low Birth Weight."
	4. "SURGEON GENERAL'S WARNING: Cigarette Smoke Contains Carbon Monoxide."

[a] All warnings wording is specified by legislation. See 15 U.S.C. §§ 1331-1341 (1982).

The objective of hazard warnings shouldn't be to deter smoking behaviour, irrespective of the truth. Overly alarmist warnings that distort the risks of smoking will undermine the credibility of the warnings effort and will potentially undermine the credibility of warnings efforts for other hazards. As I have written extensively elsewhere, hazard warnings are a valuable component of efforts to control risks in a wide variety of contexts, ranging from household chemical products to environmental exposures[3]. Honesty, credibility, and accurate dissemination of information are essential components of a responsible hazard warnings program. With these and similar efforts, it is essential to determine how consumers will process the risk information and whether warnings will in fact lead them to form accurate risk perceptions. These concerns become particularly acute with respect to the often shrill anti-smoking campaigns in the media. Likewise,

[3] See Magat and Viscusi (1992), and Viscusi and Magat (1987).

cigarette advertising should also be held to the standard that the net effect of this advertising is not to lead consumers to underassess the risks of smoking.

Cigarette advertising itself has long been a source of information regarding smoking risks. Studies indicated that as far back as the 1920's there were substantial health claims made with respect to cigarettes, which were typically of the form that this particular brand was not as dangerous for one's throat or caused less coughs and irritation than other cigarettes[4]. These health mentions in effect serve to highlight the health hazards associated with smoking by giving them increased prominence among potential consumers.

Perhaps the most vigorous advertising campaign relating to cigarette safety took place during the great tar derby of 1957-1960. During that period, cigarette companies advertised their tar and nicotine levels and competed with respect to cigarette safety. The advertising for Kent cigarettes claimed that these cigarettes had "significantly less tar and nicotine than any other filter brand." Duke cigarettes proudly claim that they have the "lowest tar of all Low-tar cigarettes," and Marlboro cigarettes had improved so that "Today's Marlboro-22% less tar, 34% less nicotine." The result of this cigarette safety competition was that within this three year period, the average tar and nicotine of the cigarettes purchased dropped by one-third.

The U.S. Federal Trade Commission banned this form of competitive advertising in 1960 in an effort that continues to reflect the government's general opposition to the use of market forces to promote cigarette safety and to permit the role of consumer choice to reduce the average riskiness of cigarettes. Indeed, the U.S. Public Health establishment recommended against smoking low tar cigarettes[5].

It wasn't until the American Cancer Society recognised the ill-conceived nature of this policy that it was reversed. The Federal Trade Commission itself published tar and nicotine levels in 1967, and in 1971 it required that all cigarette advertising include tar and nicotine levels.

The general media also provides substantial coverage of the hazards of smoking. I have compiled a tally of articles in the *Reader's Digest* beginning in 1950. Although the articles dealing with health hazards have increased over time, there has been a continuing concern over the past half century with the health risks of cigarettes, as for example the number of articles

---

[4] See Ringold and Calfee (1989).

[5] See Calfee (1985).

published in the 1980's was just under double the number of health related cigarette articles published in the 1950's[6]. The hazards of smoking are the subject of substantial public attention.

The main issue I will focus on is whether in fact this prominence has led people to perceive the risk accurately. A well established result in the literature on risk perception is that people tend to have exaggerated perceptions of the most highly publicised risks. Consequently, one would expect that this prominence would tend to lead people to overestimate the risks of smoking as compared to the true risk level. The reason for such a relationship is that media coverage does not indicate specific probabilities of risk but rather indicates the character of the danger so the effect is to simply boost probability assessments rather than to make them converge to their true value.

PERCEPTIONS OF LUNG CANCER RISKS OF SMOKING

The starting point for analysing the accuracy of the lung cancer risk perceptions will be to develop scientific reference points for these risk levels. Unfortunately, there are no published probabilities of the major health outcomes associated with smoking. The approach I adopted instead was to use the total lung cancer and death risk estimates provided by the U.S. Surgeon General, coupled with statistics on the smoking population to estimate the associated risks of smoking[7]. Thus, it is worth emphasising that these risk estimates reflect the U.S. government assessments of the hazards of smoking and do not adjust in any way for the omission of health risk factors correlated with smoking from their statistical analyses. For the survey year 1985, the lung cancer mortality risk ranged from 0.05-0.10, and for the survey year 1991 the estimate ranges from 0.06-0.13. The total mortality risk to the smoker is more than double this amount, and my current estimate of this range is from 0.18-0.36. Some rough estimates show that the lifetime mortality risk of smoking could be as high as one-third, which is currently within my estimated range.

To assess whether risk perceptions are accurate, ideally one would like quantitative information that enabled one to make a judgement as to whether people underestimate or overestimate particular hazards of smoking. Much

[6] See Viscusi (1992).

[7] The Procedures for this calculation are described in Chapter 4 of Viscusi (1992).

available survey evidence is quite qualitative in nature. For example, one of the most detailed surveys undertaken by the U.S. government focused on whether a respondent believed that the product is somewhat or very harmful[8]. Close to 100 percent of the respondents believe that tobacco products are somewhat or very harmful, which exceeds the risk belief percentages for (in order of decreasing risk) alcoholic beverages, food additives, fatty foods, artificial sweeteners, over-the-counter-drugs, and dairy products. What can we conclude from such statistics or the annual series of Gallup polls that ask smokers whether cigarette smoking is harmful? Although not completely devoid of interest, such questions do not provide a meaningful basis for determining whether people have accurate risk perceptions. What, for example, is the quantitative risk counterpart to smoking being "somewhat harmful" or "very harmful?" Not only do such measures lack any corresponding quantitative reference point for any particular individual, but to the extent that people differ with respect to the quantitative risk level that they regard as harmful then pooling the responses and making comparisons across respondent groups will not be meaningful. In a recent analysis with Anil Gaba, we found using job risk data that white-collar workers and better educated workers were more likely to regard a job as "dangerous" for any given level of objective risk than were blue-collar or less educated workers[9].

The first set of evidence regarding lung cancer risk perceptions comes from a national survey undertaken in the United States in 1985[10]. The survey was conducted by an international survey research firm, Audits & Surveys Inc. The survey was conducted using a random digit dial telephone method and included a sample of over 3000 respondents. The survey question posed the lung cancer risk question as follows: "Among 100 cigarette smokers, how many of them do you think will get lung cancer because they smoke?" Using a reference point of 100 is a convenient denominator for people to think in probability or percentage terms. I have used a similar type of population reference approach in a variety of studies of risk perception undertaken for the U.S. Environmental Protection Agency.

---

[8] These statistics are from the U.S. Bureau of Alcohol, Tobacco, and Firearms, Final Report On The Research Study Of Public Opinion Concerning Warning Labels On Containers Of Alcoholic Beverages, Dec 1988, Vol. 1, Table 2.

[9] See Gaba and Viscusi (1998).

[10] For fuller discussion of this particular survey, see Viscusi (1992).

Table II Distribution of lung cancer risk perceptions for cigarette smoking, 1985[a]

Distribution of lung cancer risk perceptions (RISK)	*Fraction with risk perceptions in interval* Full Sample	Current smokers
Risk < 0.05	.052	.092
0.05<=Risk<0.10	.046	.051
0.10<=Risk<0.20	.117	.130
0.20<=Risk<0.30	.136	.146
0.30<=Risk<0.40	.090	.114
0.40<=Risk<0.50	.052	.050
0.50<=Risk<0.60	.239	.228
0.60<=Risk<0.70	.070	.056
0.70<=Risk<0.80	.084	.050
0.80<=Risk<0.90	.042	.027
0.90<=Risk<0.99	.041	.028
Risk = 1.00	.030	.026
Mean risk	.426	.368
(standard error of mean)	(.005)	(.009)
Sample size	3,119	779

[a] Among 100 Cigarette Smokers, how many of then do you think will get lung cancer because they smoke? ("if don't know," PROBE: "Just your best guess will do").

Table II reports the distribution of the responses for the sample overall as well as current smokers. Overall, the lung cancer risk perceptions are quite substantial – with an average lung cancer risk of 0.43 for the population overall and 0.37 for current smokers. People overestimate the lung cancer risk of smoking by several times. Moreover, there appear to be very few individuals who are in categories that one might regard as being uninformed. For example, only 5 percent of the population and 9 percent of all smokers believe that the lung cancer risk probability is under 0.05.

Elsewhere I have analysed in detail the age differences in these smoking risk beliefs. Respondents in the younger age groups assessed the risks as being greater than do the older respondents. Although the findings are fairly similar for the overall different smoking status populations, let us focus on the sub-group of greatest interest, that of current smokers. Smokers in the age group 16-21 believe that the lung cancer risk probability is 0.45, as compared to 0.23 for smokers ages 22-45 and 0.33 for smokers aged 46 and over. These findings are of particular pertinence to the extent that there are policy concerns with ensuring that the younger groups are informed of the hazards of smoking. Moreover, the findings are of economic interest since they are reflective of the changing informational environment with respect to cigarette smoking risks.

Although the assessed risks of smoking are considerable, one might nevertheless question the meaningfulness of these responses. For example, one might speculate that although people believe that smoking would cause lung cancer, they may not believe that such lung cancers would be fatal. To test for this hypothesis, I undertook a local telephone survey of 206 respondents in 1991. For the full sample, the lung cancer fatality risk probability was 0.38, and for current smokers it was 0.31. This sample was not nationally representative. Indeed, it was undertaken in a leading tobacco-producing state in the United States, North Carolina, which should lead to underestimation of the risk. Nevertheless, there appeared to be substantial lung cancer mortality risk perceptions.

A potential shortcoming of these results is that they pertain only to lung cancer. Lung cancer was the first risk highlighted by the government, and it is likely that people tend to have a more of an exaggerated sense of the lung cancer risk perception than they would of any other less publicized hazards of smoking. Thus, a more comprehensive perspective on smoking risks would be obtained by focusing on the overall assessed mortality associated with smoking as opposed to the risks of any particular disease.

PERCEPTION OF THE MORTALITY RISK OF SMOKING

To determine if people have a more comprehensive perspective on smoking risks, I developed a risk question that would be the analogue of the lung cancer risk question discussed previously. In my 1991 North Carolina survey I pose the mortality question as follows: "Among 100 cigarette smokers, how many of them do you think will die from lung cancer, heart disease, throat cancer, and all other illnesses because they smoke?" The wording of this question should be sufficient to elicit a more comprehensive perspective on the hazards of smoking without the potential upward biases that could be generated by eliciting mortality risk perceptions for each individual disease specifically. The comprehensive approach also focuses on what is of paramount importance, which is the overall probability of death, rather than whether people understand each particular risk. For example, if subjects underestimate the risk of death from throat cancer, but overestimate the risk of death from lung cancer, the main policy issue of concern is whether the overall mortality risk assessment is accurate. It is unlikely that any productive role would be served through a hazard warnings effort that enabled people to better distinguish the components contributing to the mortality risk probability assuming that they correctly understood the overall risk associated with smoking.

The mortality risk assessments in the 1991 regional survey paralleled those of the lung cancer risk perceptions, but did not reflect the same extent of risk overestimation. Overall, the full sample had an average mortality risk assessment of 0.54, with current smokers believing the mortality risk was 0.47. The other population segments all believe that the risk of death was at least a 50-50 proposition. Current nonsmokers assessed the risk as 0.56, former smokers assessed the risk at 0.50, and those who had never smoked assessed the risk as being 0.59. Comparison of these estimates with the risk range in Table III indicate that the mortality risk assessments are typically twice as great as the midpoint of the estimated mortality risk to smokers and also considerably higher than the upper bound mortality risk to smokers. Indeed, all these estimates are at least as high as the estimated overall mortality risk to society, which includes outcomes such as fetal death and injuries due to fires.

Table III Actual smoking risk ranges in 1985 and 1991 for cigarette smoking

Survey Years	**Lung cancer mortality risk**	**Total mortality risk to smoker**	**Total mortality risk to society**
1985	.05-.10	.16-.32	.21-.42
1991, 1997	.06-.13	.18-.36	.23-.46

Source: Viscusi (1992), p. 70.

PERCEPTIONS OF LIFE EXPECTANCY LOSS

Even if smokers understand the probability that they may die because of their cigarette smoking, they may nevertheless fail to appreciate the extent of life that will be lost. To examine this possibility, I explored the degree to which individuals would perceive a life expectancy loss as a result of their smoking behaviour.

Table IV reports the results for the life expectancy analysis that I undertook in the 1991 North Carolina survey. The particular question I devised was the following: "The average life expectancy of a 21 year old male (female) is that he (she) will live for another 53 (59) years. What do you think the life expectancy is for the average male (female) smoker?" Thus, the question attempts to normalise the respondents based on a specific reference individual. In addition, it gives them information regarding the remaining life expectancy, so in answering a life expectancy question for smokers, the respondent does not have to simultaneously estimate what the normal life expectancy is and also determine how much of that life expectancy would be lost. Rather, the respondent can focus on the single matter of concern, which is the incremental effect of smoking behaviour. Since smokers tend to be less well educated than nonsmokers and might have a less accurate assessment of normal life expectancy, providing this information will eliminate a source of error that will not be symmetric across the smoking and non-smoking populations.

Table IV Respondent's assessed life-expectancy loss due to smoking, 1991

	Mean (standard error of the mean)		
Sample	**Males**	**Females**	**Total**
Full sample	8.5 (0.9)	13.2 (0.9)	11.5 (0.7)
Current smokers	6.9 (1.2)	10.9 (3.0)	9.0 (1.7)
Current nonsmokers	9.1 (1.2)	13.7 (0.9)	12.3 (0.7)
Former smokers	6.5 (2.4)	13.2 (1.6)	10.8 (1.1)
Never smoked	10.8 (1.1)	13.9 (1.1)	13.0 (0.8)

In terms of a reference point of the life expectancy loss, available scientific evidence indicates that it is in the range of 3.6-7.2 years[11]. As the estimates in Table IV indicate, both the full sample of males and females overestimate even the upper bound of the assessed life expectancy loss, with an average life expectancy loss estimate overall of 11.5 years. Current smokers assess

[11] For a detailed discussion of the underlying scientific evidence regarding life expectancy loss, see p. 80 Viscusi (1992).

an average life expectancy loss of 9.0 years, with the estimated life expectancy loss for male current smokers being 6.9 years and for female smokers 10.9 years. Current nonsmokers have a higher assessed life expectancy loss, with people who have never smoked having the highest life expectancy loss assessed, as one would expect.

CONCLUSION

U.S. public policy towards smoking in many respects resembles particularly unimaginative offensive strategies for sports teams. Irrespective of the success of particular plays, a team may continually run the same offensive strategy whether it works or not. In much the same way, for over three decades the principal public health strategy has been to inform smokers that cigarette smoking is risky. While smoking is enormously risky, this fundamental message is almost universally understood. It is not private information possessed only by anti-smoking zealots and the public health community.

What has been absent from the government strategy in the United States has been an effort to exploit these forces by publicising the differential hazards of alternative cigarettes and promoting innovative cigarette designs. The attitude toward such efforts is reflected in the opposition to tar and nicotine advertising when it was first begun by the industry. Since that time, the Surgeon General has attacked the smokeless cigarette, and innovations such as the de-nicotined cigarette and smoking boxes have been greeted with indifference, ridicule, and spirited opposition. The policy approach that I am advocating here and have advocated elsewhere is that the government instead should adopt a stance of rating the comparative hazard of cigarettes so that smokers can best match the riskiness of their smoking decisions to their own willingness to bear risk. This approach will not only exploit the powerful potential role of the market, but also will reflect the legitimate right consumers have to make informed risky decisions.

REFERENCES

Calfee, J.E. (1985), *Cigarette Advertising, Health Information and Regulation Before 1970*, FTC working paper, No. 134.

Gaba, A. and Viscusi, W.K. (1998), "Differences in Subjective Risk Thresholds: Worker Groups as an Example", *Management Science*, Vol. 44, No. 6, pp. 801-811.

Magat, W.A. and Viscusi, W.K. (1992), *Informational Approaches to Regulation*, MIT University Press, Cambridge.

Ringold, D.J. and Calfee, J.E. (1989), "The Informational Content of Cigarette Advertising: 1926-1986," *Journal of Public Policy and Management*, Vol. 8, pp. 1-23.

Viscusi, W.K. (1990), "Do Smokers Underestimate Risk?", *Journal of Political Economy*, Vol. 98, No. 6, pp. 1253-1269.

Viscusi, W.K. (1991), "Age Variations in Risk Perceptions and Smoking Decisions", *Review of Economics and Statistics*, Vol. 73, pp. 577-588.

Viscusi, W.K. (1992), *Smoking: Making The Risky Decision*, Oxford University Press, New York.

Viscusi, W.K. (1995), "Cigarette Taxation and the Social Consequences of Smoking", in: Poterba, J. (Ed.), *Tax Policy and the Economy,* National Bureau of Economic Research, Vol. 9, pp. 51-101.

Viscusi, W.K. (forthcoming), "Constructive Cigarette Regulation", *Duke Law Journal.*

Viscusi, W.K. and Magat, W.A. (1987), *Learning about Risk: Consumer and Worker Responses to Hazard Information,* Harvard University Press, Cambridge.

11

COMMENTARY ON PUBLIC PERCEPTION OF SMOKING RISKS

PETER ZWEIFEL

Professor Viscusi's paper presents a well-argued challenge to conventional tobacco policy, which is based on the premise that only public health specialists are able to understand and communicate smoking risks. His argument draws on excellent, innovative research he has conducted over many years. This commentary's main objective therefore is to call attention to some possibly startling policy implications of his research. Its first part repeats the findings that are of particular relevance for policy. Its second part discusses tobacco policy as an instrument for internalizing the external costs associated with smoking. Its third part points out the implications of Professor Viscusi's plea for more accurate information about the health risks of smoking. Part four concludes.

THE INFORMATION GAP

In our everyday lives, we tend to be critical of the information content of private advertising. One of the insights of Professor Viscusi's paper is that public warnings against smoking may be quite low in information content, too. In fact, he shows that these warnings fail to address the information gaps (potential) smokers may have. Specifically, the advertisements shown in table 2 of this paper lack the probability information that is necessary for reaching optimal decisions about smoking under conditions of risk.

Another highlight is the fact that risks of smoking are overestimated. While total mortality risk to smokers does not exceed 36 percent in the United States, it is estimated at 50 percent by the public and still 42 percent by smokers themselves. And while the life expectancy loss of smokers does not exceed 7.2 years, it is believed to be 8.5 years by males and even 13.2 years by females.

These discrepancies are of importance because risk beliefs do influence smoking behavior. Thus, accurate information about lung cancer risk would cause U.S. smoking rates to increase.

RATIONALE FOR GOVERNMENT ACTION

The three economic rationales for government intervention are increasing returns to scale (resulting in natural monopolies), the existence of public goods, and external costs. The first rationale can be dismissed in the present context. The second has relevance here because once information is gathered, it can be shared at almost no extra cost. At the same time, the producer of the information cannot easily sell it because he would have to disclose its contents to a potential purchaser. In this situation, there is a case for the government's financing (not necessarily producing and divulging) of information. However, Professor Viscusi makes it quite clear that in the case of the health risks of smoking, this task could be performed in a far more effective way.

In the following, this commentary focuses on the third rationale, viz. tobacco policy as an instrument for internalizing the external costs of smoking. External costs arise whenever a third party is harmed by some activity without the party carrying on the activity having to take this into due account. Specifically, smokers may not have to bear the costs caused by environmental tobacco smoke, by fires, and accidents. Thus, the dependency potential of tobacco does not constitute an external cost to the extent that its consequences in terms of illness and premature death are largely borne by the smoking individual himself. It is through public welfare programmes and even more importantly through social health insurance whose contributions are not risk-rated that we allow some of these costs to be shifted to society. Since the costs of premature death fall on the smokers themselves while constituting the major part of total economic cost of smoking (according to the estimates in this volume), the external costs of smoking are substantially lower than suggested by the total figures.

The logic of tobacco policy as an internalizing instrument is presented in Figure I. There, the private marginal cost of tobacco smoking (MC_p) is assumed to be constant, whereas marginal external cost (MC_e) is shown increasing in the amount of tobacco consumed. This reflects the assumption of an endemic effect: The more smoking there is, the more additional consumers will catch on, adding to environmental smoke and hence the burden of external cost. Thus, social marginal cost of tobacco smoking (MC_s) increases in the quantity consumed (Q) as well. The demand function (D'F') reflects the status quo, with rather incomplete and inaccurate information provided to smokers. It is drawn responsive to price because the evidence presented by Professor Chaloupka in this volume indicates that even with dependence the elasticity of demand w.r.t. price is nonzero.

The market equilibrium is determined by the equality of marginal willingness to pay by consumers (as given by the demand function) and private marginal cost (MC_p). This occurs at point E_p, with consumption at Q_p. Optimally, however, equilibrium should be at point E', where marginal willingness to pay equals social marginal cost (MC_s). From an efficiency point of view, one would be hard put to deny someone the pleasure of smoking, provided he or she covers the extra social cost caused by so doing. Still, internalization of the external cost calls for a reduction of tobacco consumption, from Q_p to Q' in Figure I. This reduction can be brought about in three ways.

(a) Tobacco consumption may be regulated, e.g. by prohibition of smoking in public rooms and by minors.

(b) An internalizing tax at the tune of t may be imposed, causing private marginal cost to increase (from OG to OG', resulting in equilibrium at E' in Figure I).

(c) Smoking permits covering the amount of Q' may be created (or, equivalently, cigarettes rationed at Q'). In Figure I, MC_p becomes vertical at point K' again resulting in equilibrium at E'.

Given the rather heavy taxation of cigarettes in industrial countries, emphasis will be on the internalizing tax in the following.

Figure I True risk information and (efficient) tobacco policy

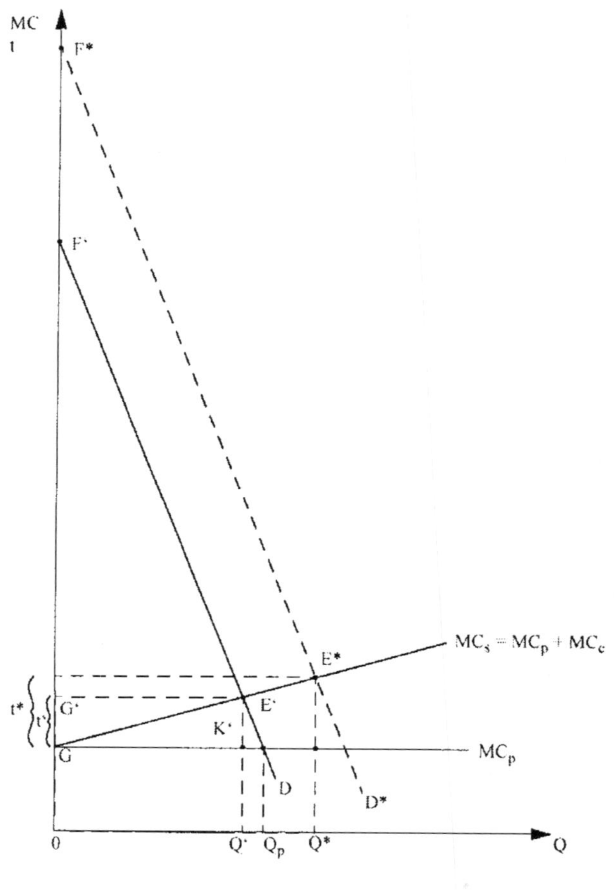

THE UNEXPECTED OUTCOME OF AN INTERNALIZATION POLICY

The plea of Professor Viscusi, calling for more accurate information about smoking risks, is likely to meet with a favorable response from all parties concerned. However, accurate information may well have unexpected consequences for a tobacco policy seeking to internalize the external costs of smoking. Recall that accurate information would increase the smoking rate in the United States. The cause of this increase is the revised risk information, resulting in a higher demand for cigarettes. In terms of Figure I, this means that the demand curve shifts out from D'F' to D*F*. Equality of marginal willingness to pay and social marginal cost now occurs at point E*. This transition is associated with five different effects.

(1) **An increase of the optimal rate of taxation**. This will be noted with satisfaction by proponents of an activist tobacco policy. In Figure I, the increase is from t' to t*.

(2) **An increase in tobacco consumption** (given that the initial level was efficient). This will be greeted with much less enthusiasm by most public health specialists. Assuming the point of departure was E', the marginal cost function MC_s would have to run vertical (which it does not) to keep consumption constant. In order to exclude an increase in tobacco consumption, one would have to argue that present smoking rates are still far excessive due to failure of taxation to internalize external cost. This is not very credible in view of the rather high rates of taxation (see e.g. the contribution by Professor Barendregt in this volume). Therefore, the assumed transition will be from E' to E* for the remainder of the argument.

(3) **An increase in the net benefit enjoyed by smokers**. This may be quite upsetting for any policy maker holding paternalistic views. The shift of the demand curve from D'F' to D*F* implies that total willingness to pay (the area under the demand curve) increases. The area above the price paid is the net benefit to smokers (called consumer surplus). In Figure I, this surplus increases, from area E'F'G' to area E*F*G*.

(4) **An increase in the total external cost of smoking borne by society**. This implication of an efficiency oriented tobacco policy is hard to accept by all those affected by the external effects of smoking, in particular environmental smoke. However, it is the necessary consequence of an increase in the quantity of tobacco products consumed. In Figure I, the area between the social and the private marginal cost functions measures the total external cost borne by society. This area increases from GE'K' to GE*K*.

(5) **An increase in the revenue from the taxation of tobacco**. This implication will please tobacco policy activists to the extent that there is more funding for their activities. It offers little consolation to those affected by effect No. (4) because as a rule the additional tax revenue is used for general government purposes rather than for compensating them. In Figure I, tax revenue is given by the area GK'E'G' in the initial situation and by GK*E*G* after the dissemination of more accurate risk information.

ALTERNATIVE POLICY APPROACHES

In sum, Professor Viscusi's plea for more accurate information about the health risks of smoking makes good sense. Apart from the intrinsic value of truth, it enhances economic efficiency. However, if embedded in an efficiency oriented tobacco policy, better information has the disturbing feature of resulting in higher cigarette consumption, with only the smokers profiting from the efficiency gain. This goes a long way in explaining the hesitation of health policy makers to make tobacco warnings more informative and accurate. With this insight, serious consideration should be given to the possibilities of reducing the external costs of smoking mentioned in Professor Viscusi's contribution, such as the smokeless cigarette or the de-nicotined cigarette.

12

RISK, RATIONALITY AND THE CONSUMPTION OF TOBACCO[1]

ANIL MARKANDYA

INTRODUCTION

Everyone acknowledges that the consumption of tobacco is a risky activity. Like many other risky activities it is undertaken by a lot of individuals. In this sense it is not surprising that people continue to smoke after being warned about the risks; they also continue to partake in dangerous sports, and to consume other products that are dangerous but society does not make such a serious effort to stop them. Why then, does smoking receive such attention from policy-makers? I would argue that there are three reasons for this. By far the most important is the view that smoking is irrational. Rationality involves the pursuit of a consistent objective or set of objectives, taking full account of all information available at the time the decisions are made. Policy makers are of the view that smokers are too easily persuaded by the advertisers and by peer group norms about the desirability of smoking, and that once they have started, smoking changes their habits or preferences. Hence their decision to continue is no longer 'rational'. Rationality would require that they took account of this habit-forming aspect

[1] I would like to thank the participants of the conference on the Social Costs of Smoking, held in Lausanne in August 1998 for helpful comments on an earlier draft. Thanks are also due to my colleagues Pamela Mason and Paul Heap for some guidance on the literature. All errors are, of course, mine.

when they first started, and there is little evidence, they argue, that this is the case[2].

The second reason why smoking receives such attention is the 'external effect' aspect of smoking, or passive smoking. One person's smoke causes damage to another person and this damage is not taken into account when the smoker makes his or her decision to smoke. This aspect of smoking control requires the policy-maker to estimate the external costs and to ensure that they are passed on to the smoker. The estimation of such costs will also influence policies towards control, such as limiting smoking in public places. Although an important aspect of policy in this area, this paper is not concerned with passive smoking.

Finally social policy focuses on smoking because of its high costs to the health service and to the economy. Individuals who consume tobacco make greater demands on health facilities[3] and take more time off work. Smokers argue that the taxes they pay on tobacco more than make up for these costs and so they have paid their debt to society. Whether or not this is the case is debatable, but again this paper does not focus primarily on this issue.

The main interest in this paper is, therefore, to understand what a rational strategy for tobacco consumption would look like and how it would respond to external incentives, such as taxes, or awareness programmes. Some work has been done on this over the years. In particular, Ippolito (1981) raised the very same question, asking how tobacco consumption would change over a lifetime in a model in which the individual was maximising lifetime expected utility over a fixed time period or life span. Her model was, however, limited in some respects (in each period income equalled consumption so there was no borrowing or lending) and she did not look at the consumption paths arising from plausible parameter values and different risk perceptions. Viscusi (1992) worked within the rational paradigm and made a strong case for it as a tool for explaining long term smoking trends. Others have also modelled consumption under risk but there are very few attempts to explain smoking from a lifetime viewpoint.

---

[2] All these reasons for irrationality give rise to the 'merit good' argument, by which society deems it appropriate to discourage the consumption of several health-impairing goods.

[3] Over a lifetime it is not clear that smokers do in fact 'cost' the health services more. For detailed calculations on this question see the paper by Barendregt in this volume.

An alternative approach that has been developed in the health economics literature models the intertemporal consumption of goods in terms of their impacts on life span. Goods are divided into 'healthy, 'unhealthy' and 'neutral'. The consumption of healthy goods increases life span while unhealthy goods' consumption does the reverse (Ried, 1998; Grossman, 1998; Forster, 1997). Although this approach has some promise, it has not been applied to tobacco consumption. I would argue that it is less suitable for modelling tobacco than Ippolito's framework. With tobacco it is less an issue of extending life span than one of changing the probabilities of survival within a given life span (one that has remained remarkably stable for a long period of time).

This paper investigates the decisions that would be made by a rational individual, taking account of the effects that smoking has both on utility as well as on the probability of survival in the future. The basic model, which follows Ippolito's approach, is set out in Section 2 – Modelling rational consumption – of the paper. Section 3 – Tobacco consumption affects survival probabilities – reports the results for a specific set of functions and survival probabilities. These are only indicative but more detailed analysis by the author confirms that they are broadly correct. Section 4 looks at how the consumption paths are affected by habit formation, by changes in risk perception and other factors. Section 5 concludes the paper with a discussion of how these results effect our perception of the social costs of tobacco consumption and what relevance they have for policy.

MODELLING RATIONAL CONSUMPTION

The conventional method in economics of modelling decision-making under risk is that of expected utility maximisation. Starting from a few simple axioms of rationality, von Neumann and Morgernstern (1944) showed that choices under risk could be ordered using an expected utility rule, where the expected utility is the sum of the probabilities of different, mutually exclusive, events, multiplied by the utility attached to those events. The rule postulates the existence of a utility function, the shape of which reflects the individual's attitude to risk.

With smoking, the framework is best represented with a utility function in which utility in period 'i' is given by:

$$U^i = U^i(C_i, S_i) \tag{1}$$

C_i = consumption of other goods in period i;
S_i = amount smoked in period i.

Let d_i be the probability that the individual will die at the end of period i. Assume further that the individual has a maximum life span of T periods. By definition,

$$\sum_i d_i = 1 \tag{2}$$

The expected utility for a person dying in period 'i' is:

$$d_i \sum_{j<i} U^j(C_j, S_j) \tag{3}$$

By adding terms and rearranging, it can be shown that the expected utility overall period is:

$$\sum_{j=1}^{j=T} \Pi^j U^j(C_j, S_j) \tag{4}$$

where Π^j is the survival probability and is defined as

$$\Pi^j = (1 - d_1 - d_2 - d_{(j-1)}) \tag{5}$$

Equation (4) is the function to be maximised. The constraint to the maximisation is intertemporal: lifetime consumption equals lifetime income.

Excluding discounting[4], which is not central to the analysis, the budget constraint can be written as:

$$\sum_{i=1}^{i=T}(C_i + P_i S_i) - M = 0 \tag{6}$$

P_i is the price of a unit of smoking and M is disposable lifetime income. One can think of this income as being the conversion of an uncertain actual income stream into a fixed lump sum, which represent the present value of the individuals permanent income, and from which an annuity can be purchased[5]. The maximisation problem consists of maximising (4) subject to (6). The structure also assumes that the individual places no value on bequests. Given uncertain future consumption, premature death will result in incomplete consumption plans. The optimal consumption plans ensure, by construction, that the individual will never be in debt at the time of death.

THE BENCHMARK CASE

The benchmark case is taken as one in which the survival probabilities are independent of the amount smoked. In that case it is easily shown that the optimal consumption path must satisfy:

$$\frac{U_S^j}{U_C^j} = P_j \qquad \text{for all j} \tag{7}$$

$$\Pi^j U_C^j = \Pi^l U_C^l$$

$$\Pi^j U_S^j = \Pi^l U_S^l \qquad \text{for all time periods j and l} \tag{8}$$

Equation (7) states that the marginal rate of substitution between the consumption good and tobacco remains equal to the price of smoking in all

---

[4] Discount rates, however, do have an effect on the results. The higher the rate, the less impact there will be on smoking patterns of the future risks of present day smoking.

[5] The model ignores the fact that this permanent income may be affected by smoking. Such effects can be modelled but at the cost of a considerable increase in the complexity of the analysis. Moreover, as is argued later, the consequences of such a link are only to reinforce the conclusions of this paper, which can be brought out more starkly with a fixed income assumption.

periods[6]. This result is independent of the risks of tobacco consumption and is standard in any static economic analysis of consumer behaviour.

Equations (8) state that the marginal expected utility from consumption of either good must be equal across all time periods.

This simple decision-making problem can be characterised as a two-stage process. First the consumer chooses S_i and C_i as a function of income allocated to period 'i', which can be set at Y_i. This makes utility in period i a function of the price in that period (P_i) and income (Y_i) and the resulting function is called the indirect utility function. The second stage chooses Y_i as a result of maximising utility subject to the constraint that the sum of Y_i equal M.

A special case of the above problem is one where the utility function is of the Cobb-Douglas form:

$$U^i = \log(C_i^{\alpha}, S_i^{1-\alpha}) \quad 0<\alpha<1 \tag{9}$$

For this form it is easy to show that the indirect utility function is:

$$U^i = k(\alpha) + \log Y_i + (\alpha - 1)\log P_i \tag{10}$$

k is a constant (function of α). The problem now is to maximise

$$\sum_i \Pi^i U^i \qquad \text{subject to} \qquad \sum_i Y_i = M \tag{11}$$

This gives the condition that Y_i is proportional to the survival probability Π^i, which implies that income allocated to each period is proportional to the survival probability, with the factor of proportionality dependent on the price of smoking (P_i). This result is, of course dependent on the particular function chosen. Not only is it dependent on the Cobb-Douglas form, but on the particular transformation chosen. Since in expected utility framework the utility function is cardinal, the log transform in (9) is critical. Other

[6] The 'price' includes, in addition to the market price, any costs of smoking borne by the smoker. These may be the health costs of smoking-related illnesses. This is discussed later on in the paper.

transforms would result in allocations of Y_i over time that were substantially different from that given here[7].

For the purposes of the benchmark analysis the log form of the Cobb-Douglas utility function has been retained. Although the latter implies unit price and income elasticities for tobacco consumption, which is not in conformity with the empirical evidence, the gains in analytical insight outweigh the loss of empirical accuracy from taking this form[8].

In order to illustrate smoking patterns over time when no account is taken of the effects of tobacco consumption on survival probabilities, Π^i has been set for seven periods, each representing a decade, from 15-25, to 75-85. The data are given in Table I and represent a life expectancy at birth of 70 years. Data are taken from EU demographic statistics. Lifetime income is set at 700 units, so that average income per decade is normalised at 100. For further simplicity P_i is set at one for all periods. The parameter $\forall$ is set at 0.975, so that 2.5 percent of income would be allocated to tobacco consumption in a one period utility maximising framework. This is broadly consistent with the allocation of income to tobacco for an average smoker.

Table I shows very small declines in tobacco consumption for the first six decades (about 6 percent), followed by a slightly bigger decline in the last decade (about 17 percent). This pattern is mainly determined by the survival probabilities. If the price were to increase in all periods, the allocation of income would not change across periods, although smoking in each time period would decline. If the price of smoking increased with time, tobacco consumption would decline correspondingly. An interesting policy aspect would be to see how health-related costs, borne by the consumer, would decrease tobacco consumption as a function of time.

---

[7] The cardinalisation of the function $U(.)$ is represented by the transform $(1/(1-\gamma))U^{(1/(1-\gamma))}$. In the limit when γ tends to one, the function tends to log ($U(.)$), which is the transform taken here. The higher the value of γ the more concave the utility function and the more risk averse the behaviour.

[8] Viscusi (1992) reports price elasticities for smoking of between –0.4 and –1.4, with the higher values applying to younger smokers. Long term elasticities are higher than short term ones, which is consistent with the empirical and theoretical literature on consumer behaviour.

Table 1 Lifetime distribution of smoking

Period	Age	Tobacco Consumption	Other Consumption	Survival Probability	Expected Utility
1	20	3.14	122.53	0.998	112.54
2	30	3.10	121.06	0.986	109.58
3	40	3.08	119.95	0.977	105.18
4	50	2.55	112.95	0.920	95.60
5	60	1.84	99.32	0.809	73.92
6	70	1.84	71.70	0.584	38.65
7	80	0.90	34.99	0.285	7.17
Total		17.5	682.5		

Note:

1. The survival probabilities are the conditional probabilities of being alive at the beginning of the period.
2. Since the price of tobacco in consumption terms is set at one the units of tobacco can be interpreted as the expenditure on tobacco per decade out of the total income of 100 per decade.

TOBACCO CONSUMPTION AFFECTS SURVIVAL PROBABILITIES

The case when tobacco consumption affects survival probabilities can be expressed as the following constrained maximisation problem in which the maximand is ℓ . ℓ is defined as.

$$\ell = \sum_i \Pi^i U^i + \lambda \sum_i (C_i + S_i) - M \tag{12}$$

The first order conditions give, for all i:

$$\Pi^i U_C^i - \lambda = 0 \tag{13}$$

$$\Pi^i U_S^i + \sum_{j>i} U^j \frac{\partial \Pi^j}{\partial S_i} - \lambda P_i \tag{14}$$

From (13) we get the result

$$\Pi^i U_C^i = \Pi^j U_C^j \tag{15}$$

As for the benchmark case. From (13) and (14) we get

$$\frac{U_C^i}{U_S^i} + \frac{1}{\Pi^i U_C^i} \sum_{j>i} U^j \frac{\partial \Pi^j}{\partial S_i} = P_i \tag{16}$$

Since $\partial \Pi^i / \partial S_i < 0$, comparing (7) and (16) shows that the marginal rate of substitution between smoking and consumption is higher than in the benchmark case. Figure I illustrates the shift in S_i when the effects of tobacco consumption on survival probabilities are taken into account. Of course there is no guarantee that S_{ib} and S_{io} will be on the same indifference curve. The full analysis of changes in S_i and C_i requires the solution of the system of equations (13) and (14), subject to income constraint (6)[9].

It is clear, however, that the lower the value of i (the earlier in the lifetime), the greater will be the absolute value of the second term in (16), and hence the greater the shift to the left on the indifference curve I_1.

[9] With homothetic preferences, the values of the marginal rate of substitution are constant on any ray from the origin. In that case the ratio of C/S will increase relative to the benchmark case, and this result holds independently of changes in the level of optimal utility. This holds in the case of the Cobb-Douglas utility function.

Figure I *Consumption and smoking choices*

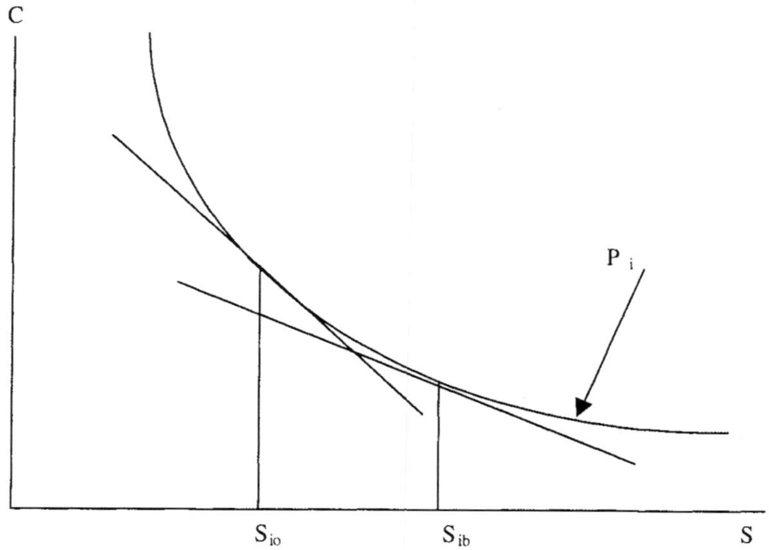

S_{ib} = benchmark case
S_{io} = 'tobacco affects survival probability' case

For a numerical simulation of the above model we return to the Cobb-Douglas function (9) of the previous section. The equivalent of equations (13) and (14) now becomes:

$$\frac{\Pi^i}{C^i} = \frac{\Pi^j}{C^j} \tag{17}$$

$$\frac{U_C^i}{U_S^i} + \frac{C_i}{\Pi^i} \sum_{j>i} U^j \frac{\partial \Pi^j}{\partial S_i} = P_i \tag{18}$$

For the numerical simulations we take the following form of the survival probability function:

$$\Pi^j (S_1, S_2, \ldots . S_{j-1}) = \Pi_0^j e^{\sum_{i>j} k_{ij} S_i} \tag{19}$$

This has the property that when the level of smoking is zero the survival probabilities are the same as in the benchmark case. The values of k_{ij} are -

empirically determined, with the interpretation that a unit increase in smoking in period 'i' reduces the survival probability in period 'j' by the amount k_{ij}.

Using the specific form for Π^j from (19) in equation (18) provides a system of equations that can be estimated by non-linear methods. The results are given in Table II, along with the corresponding values of k_{ij}, which are given in Table III.

Table II Optimal smoking in the case where tobacco affects survival probability

		Optimal Consumption			**Benchmark Case**	
Period	Mean Age	Tobacco Cons.	Other Cons.	Survival Prob.	Tobacco Cons.	Survival Prob.
1	20	0.21	123.5	0.998	2.60	1.000
2	30	0.22	121.9	0.978	2.60	0.999
3	40	0.26	119.4	0.954	2.59	0.996
4	50	0.31	113.9	0.906	2.58	0.992
5	60	0.45	100.1	0.792	2.55	0.981
6	70	0.79	72.4	0.565	2.42	0.931
7	80	0.80	31.2	0.241	2.16	0.831

Table III Values of k_{ij}

Period	**1**	**2**	**3**	**4**	**5**	**6**
1	-0.030	-0.0150	-0.0075	-0.00375	-0.00180	-0.00094
2		-0.0300	-0.0150	-0.00750	-0.00375	-0.00180
3			-0.0300	-0.01500	-0.00750	-0.00375
4				-0.03000	-0.01500	-0.00750
5					-0.03000	-0.01500
6						-0.03000

The values of k_{ij} are set so that, with no adjustment to the amount smoked with respect to the benchmark case, life expectancy declines by 7 years, from 70 to 63. This is roughly consistent with the evidence on smoking. The implied elasticity of survival probability with respect to smoking is around –

0.1. The rate at which effects of smoking 'wear off' is 50% per decade. This last estimate is speculative and needs to be confirmed.

The changes in smoking are very large when account is taken of these survival probabilities. Smoking falls by around 90% in the first period, and by similar amounts in periods 2-5. In period 6 the fall is about 80% and in the final period there is no fall. That is, of course, the result of the fact that smoking in the last period has no effect on survival probabilities. In a model with more periods, this effect would be much smaller.

The result of the reduction in smoking is to restore life expectancy to 69 years. In other words, the smoker 'gives up' one year of life expectancy for the pleasure of smoking, but the amount smoked is very much less than it would be if no account was taken of the mortality effects of smoking.

The above model was estimated for different values of the k_{ij}. The results are quite insensitive to the values taken for these parameters, with the plausible range. *The rational response to including the mortality effects of smoking is to reduce consumption by a large amount, especially in periods 1-5 (ages 15-65).* This effect would be even stronger if the feedback loop from smoking on lifetime income, which has been excluded from the analysis, were to be included. Finally it is also interesting to note that smoking goes up slightly with age, even excluding the last period for which, as has been noted, the effect is somewhat artificial.

It should also be noted that the above results are somewhat stronger than in previous work. They suggest that, moving from no allowance for tobacco consumption on survival probabilities, to a full allowance based on mortality risks that are currently considered correct, should have a major impact on consumption. Viscusi (1992) estimated that individual perceptions of risk of tobacco consumption were much higher than those justified by the empirical evidence. He calculated that a fall in the perceived relative mortality effect from 43 percent to 5-10% (which was what the scientific evidence in 1985 indicated as the appropriate range) would result in an increase in the rate of smoking across all groups from 6.5 percent to 7.5 percent. The assumed relative risks of tobacco consumption in the above model are about 10-15 percent, but the model indicates that anyone who would have smoked around 20 cigarettes a day when no risk (zero percent relative mortality effect) was associated with consumption should virtually give up with the present risk. Although I have not run the model with the risk changes from Viscusi, it would be very surprising if the expected fall in consumption in going from a 43 percent relative mortality impact to a 5-10 percent one would not be much bigger.

SOME FURTHER CONSIDERATIONS

The above model provides a basis for the analysis of various effects and policy variables. Before discussing these it is worth pointing out that a more careful estimation of the parameters of the above model is warranted. What has been presented is only indicative of the way in which risk and tobacco consumption preferences affect the pattern of lifetime tobacco consumption. Data from household expenditure surveys, or even better from longitudinal surveys, can be used to estimate the utility and risk parameters on the assumption that smoking is rationally determined. If the estimated values are consistent with other studies of the same parameters, that provides some evidence that a rationally determined smoking model is a reasonable basis for policy analysis.

Addiction

One important factor that has to be added to the model is addiction. From the model analysed here I conclude that rational behaviour alone cannot explain the continued levels of tobacco consumption. Although there have been significant falls, they have not been as large as the model would suggest. Viscusi (1995) reports on US data for 50 years from 1944. Allowing for the lower tar content of cigarettes, *per capita* consumption has fallen by about 80 percent over that period. Rational behaviour as modelled above would suggest a drop of twice that amount; more if the effect of smoking on reducing lifetime permanent income were taken into account. Thus while the rational model does surprisingly well, it does not tell the whole story. The difference can be explained by the fact that either smokers are not well informed about the risks, or that they fail to account for the addictive effects of smoking. As has been noted above, smokers appear to *overestimate* the risks of smoking. This suggests strongly that there is an important role for addiction in explaining smoking behaviour.

There are different ways in which addiction can be defined (See Markandya and Pearce, 1989 for further discussion of this). Within this framework, the most convenient way is to make deviation from the optimal path a function of the amount smoked cumulatively. Mathematically we can write:

$$S_{ia} = S_{i0} e^{\mu \sum_{j<i} s_j} \tag{20}$$

S_{ia} is the amount smoked with addiction and the function has the property that if no smoking has occurred in previous periods, the level will be the same as it would be in the absence of any addiction effect. μ is the parameter measuring the strength of the addiction effect. A unit increase in smoking in the previous periods results in an increase in the ratio of addiction smoking to non-addiction smoking of μ percent.

For a complete estimation of the inter-temporal behaviour of a consumer, μ has to be added to the list of parameters to be estimated. In the above model that would include α, the smoking preference parameter, and γ the inequality aversion parameter. If some estimates of μ exist in the addiction literature, those can be used as a prior set of values against which the results of the above model can be compared.

It should be noted that, for the parameters used for Table II, the rational consumer might have difficulty getting addicted, since optimal consumption is very low. It would need some careful analysis of μ and possible other forms of the addiction function to see if addiction from such low levels was feasible.

Effects of new information

The optimal smoking path is based on information available in the first time period. As new information comes in, the path will be modified. The individual will re-compute the optimal path, based on the residual income and survival probabilities. In particular one is interested in the impact of changes in the last of these on the patterns of smoking. The steady increase in the evidence on the harmful effects of tobacco consumption will shift consumption downward, although the preliminary evidence suggests that the optimal paths are not very sensitive to small changes in these survival probabilities. In principle, however, the contingent paths can be modelled. What is required is data on the shifts in survival probabilities.

If the above model is valid, it suggests that information on, and an acceptance of, the risks associated with smoking would result in substantial reductions in the levels of smoking. Empirical data such as that collected by Viscusi (1995) suggests, however, that the perceived risks are higher than the objective ones, with young smokers overestimating risks even more than older ones. If individuals acted on the perceived risks, this rational model predicts that they would smoke less than they do. The problem may be a failure in understanding probabilities, particularly the complex structure of cascading effects that smoking now has on the future survival probabilities.

Changes in the price of smoking

Increasing the price of tobacco can and does reduce consumption, and governments have used this channel to influence demand. The main social concern with this policy is its regressive nature, even more so as smoking rates fall disproportionately among the better educated and the higher income groups.

The 'price' of smoking is not only the price paid for tobacco at the point of sale, but also the costs arising from health and other consequences of smoking. These include workdays lost, payments for medical care etc. In so far as such costs are an increasing function of tobacco consumption, they can be converted in a 'price' element[10]. If the effects of smoking on costs are linear, a constant price per unit smoked will apply and the above analysis remains valid. If, however, the costs are non-linearly related to smoking levels, the model becomes one of non-linear prices (see Wilson, 1993) and is more complex to solve. Even with such complexities, rational behaviour can be modelled and prediction made. The constraint is the availability of the relevant data.

POLICY IMPLICATIONS

The modelling of rational tobacco consumption is complex and demanding, both empirically and analytically. It is only worth undertaking if it provides a basis for sound policy on tobacco control. Others, notably Viscusi, have argued that there is considerable mileage to be gained from taking a rational approach. This paper supports that case. It is not possible to formulate policy measures unless one can predict individual responses to those policies. Social policy toward smoking broadly falls into the following categories:

i. Fiscal incentives (e.g. higher taxes)

ii. Awareness/information campaigns

iii. Transferring the secondary costs of smoking to individuals through contingent insurance premiums etc.

iv. Physical restriction on smoking (e.g. designated non-smoking areas).

---

[10] The other costs are likely to be especially high in the later years. This will result in less smoking with age than the model predicts.

The above model can be used to evaluate the effects of (i) to (iii) above. If target reductions in smoking rates are to be achieved, the government will need to know how individuals respond to fiscal incentives and informational programmes. Already the above model suggests that a rational response to information campaigns may be small, *to the extent that individuals have the information, understand it, and act on it.* Marginal adjustments to further data on the risks of tobacco consumption should be small. It is the understanding of the complex effects of tobacco consumption on health that is the difficult issue.

An empirical model with a sound theoretical basis is also important in estimating the individual costs of control policies. Society takes the view that smoking is to be discouraged (on merit good grounds), but the extent of such discouragement may be tempered by the costs such policies impose on individuals. Estimating these costs requires a model of individual choice, based on some assumptions of rationality.

CONCLUSIONS

To a casual observer, the modelling of tobacco consumption as a rational phenomenon may seem strange. Surely, it will be argued, smoking is a social act, which has serious adverse consequences. Smokers respond to social pressures and advertising and become addicted. Hence their behaviour is in no way rational. There are elements of truth in this view, but it does not provide a sufficient basis for understanding smoking behaviour. Smoking is a risky activity, which gives some people pleasure. Moreover, the risks of tobacco consumption are well known. Empirical evidence suggests that smoking patterns are changing as more attention is devoted to getting the message of the risks across.

It is possible to explain lifetime smoking patterns in terms of expected utility maximisation and perceived risks of smoking. These risks are complex and it is possible that many smokers misunderstand them. Information on the difference between the 'lay' and 'expert' risks of smoking is very limited. One area of useful research would be to understand how these two are related.

Stochastic lifetime consumption models of the kind analysed here do not mean that young people sit and draw up an optimal consumption plan based on the maximisation of a complex intertemporal function. Obviously they do not do that. But, just as savings behaviour can be explained by such models, so perhaps can tobacco consumption behaviour. In particular, the influence of smoking on future survival probabilities might be underestimated. This kind of model allows one to investigate that possibility and to see how changes in these perceptions can influence smoking behaviour. In that respect it is a potentially useful policy tool.

REFERENCES

Forster, M. (1997), "An Intertemporal Model of Healthy and Unhealthy Lifestyles and Optimal Lifespan", *The University of York Discussion Papers in Economics,* No. 97/13.

Grossman, M. (1998), "On the Optimal Length of Life", *Journal of Health Economics,* Vol. 17, pp. 499-509.

Ippolito, P.M. (1981), "Information and the Life Cycle Consumption of Hazardous Goods", *Economic Inquiry,* Vol. 19, pp. 529-558.

Markandya, A. and Pearce, D.W. (1989), "Measuring the Social Costs of Smoking: the Issue of Addiction", *British Journal of Addiction,* Vol. 84, pp. 1139-1150.

Ried, W. (1998), "Comparative Dynamic Analysis of the Full Grossman Model", *Journal of Health Economics,* Vol. 17, pp. 383-425.

Viscusi, W.K. (1992), *Smoking: Making the Risky Decision,* Oxford University Press, New York.

Viscusi, W.K. (1995), "Cigarette Taxation and the Social Consequences of Smoking", in: Poterba, J. (Ed.), *Tax Policy and the Economy,* National Bureau of Economic Research, Vol. 9, pp. 51-101.

Von Neumann, J. and Morgernstern, O. (1944), *The Theory of Games and Economic Behaviour,* Princeton University Press, Princeton, New Jersey.

Wilson, R.B. (1993), *Non-Linear Pricing,* Oxford University Press, New York.

13

GENDER DIFFERENCES IN THE DEMAND FOR CIGARETTES

JONI HERSCH[1]

Research suggests that at least one-fourth of regular smokers will die from smoking-related diseases (U.S. Department of Health and Human Services, 1989). In the U.S., smoking is responsible for more than one of every six deaths (U.S. Department of Health and Human Services, 1989). In most countries, men began cigarette smoking earlier than women and have a higher peak rate of use. Among users, men have tended to have higher consumption levels. For this reason, the health consequences of tobacco use have been most evident among men. Indeed, of the estimated 3 million deaths per year world-wide caused by tobacco use, only about half a million are among women (Chollat-Traquet, 1992).

While men's tobacco consumption has continued to decline substantially in most developed countries, women's tobacco use has risen in developing countries and declined more modestly in most developed countries. In some cases, tobacco use by women exceeds that of men. Women are suffering and dying from the same tobacco related diseases as men. In addition, there are health consequences of tobacco use that are unique to women. Because of health risks related to pregnancy and child raising, women's smoking

---

[1] I acknowledge with gratitude the excellent research assistance of Ekaterina Fedorova.

behaviour leads to perhaps even more critical public policy issues than those related to men.

In developed countries, the smoking rates of women are currently between 20 percent and 37 percent and are largely comparable to the smoking rates for men within their country. The smoking rates for women in developing countries are currently lower, ranging from almost no tobacco use to around 15 percent. In contrast to the pattern for developed countries, better educated and higher earning women in developing countries are more likely to smoke. Countries with the lowest smoking rates for women generally have high male smoking rates. In many developed countries, smoking patterns by women have tended to follow the male pattern of growth with a lag of 20 to 30 years. If this pattern continues in developing countries, in the future the smoking rates of men and women may become similar in developing countries as well as in developed countries.

Public health officials in a number of countries have been active in attempting to reduce smoking. The available policy tools include taxation, restrictions on smoking, and education, and these are used in varying degrees in different countries. Public health campaigns intended to reduce smoking will be most effective if the underlying individual motives for smoking are well understood. While many factors should have similar effects on smoking participation and consumption, other factors appear to differ by gender. Women in blue-collar jobs may exhibit the higher smoking rates traditionally found for men in these jobs. Further, women are far more likely than men to use cigarettes for weight management and as an outlet for stress or depression. Because the character of the preferences for smoking differs by gender, women may also differ in their response to public policy effort to reduce smoking.

To analyse the influence of these factors on smoking behaviour, I use data on approximately 48,000 individuals age 21 to 60 from the 1992 and 1993 Current Population Survey: Tobacco Use Supplement. After describing the patterns of smoking by gender and other demographic characteristics, the paper presents estimates of participation and consumption elasticities for price, family income, and employment status, separately by gender, taking into account the various influences of factors that may lead to gender differences in demand. The paper concludes with a discussion of the policy implications that arise from this analysis.

INTERNATIONAL EVIDENCE ON SMOKING RATES BY GENDER

The World Health Organisation (WHO) has tabulated smoking statistics for a number of countries around the world. Much of the following discussion is based on data from 87 countries, representing 85 percent of the world's population that provided reliable data on smoking prevalence.

Table I summarises regional statistics on smoking rates. As of the early 1990s, WHO estimates that 47 percent of the men and 12 percent of the women worldwide are daily smokers. Among more developed countries, the smoking rate for men is 42 percent; for women it is 24 percent. In less developed countries, the smoking rates are 48 percent and 7 percent for men and women, respectively. The lowest smoking rates for women are found in the countries in the African, Eastern Mediterranean, and South-East Asia regions, with smoking rates of about 4 percent in each of these regions, and about 8 percent in the Western Pacific region. In these regions, the smoking rate for men far exceed that for women, ranging from 60 percent in the Western Pacific region to about 29 percent in the African region.

Table I Estimated smoking prevalence for women and men by region

	Female rate	**Male rate**
World	12	47
More developed countries	24	42
Less developed countries	7	48
WHO Regions:		
African	4	29
American	22	35
Eastern Mediterranean	4	35
European	26	46
South-East Asia	4	44
Western Pacific	8	60

Source: World Health Organization based on most recent available data.
www.who.ch/psa/toh/Alert/apr96/gifs/table2.gif

Smoking prevalence rates vary widely by country, by gender within country, and over time within country. To provide some examples of the trends, Table II presents smoking rates in several countries provided by various sources. Taking all countries as a whole (including those not reported in the table), several points are noteworthy. First, smoking rates peaked earliest for men in developed countries and in most cases has trended downward. However, although the rate for women is below that of men in all developed countries but Denmark and Sweden, smoking rates for women have been stable or have declined more gradually than that for men in their country. Not all developed countries have experienced a decline in smoking prevalence. For example, the smoking rates for both men and women in Israel increased between 1972 and 1989; and smoking among women in Japan, Italy, and Spain has increased.

Second, in many developing countries, smoking rates for women are rising. For example, the smoking rate for women in Bangladesh was about 1 percent in 1980, but had increased to about 15 percent one decade later. During this period, the smoking rate for men declined somewhat, from 67 percent to 60 percent. Over the same period, Zaire experienced a substantial increase in smoking prevalence among both men and women. For women, the rate increased from 10 percent to 25 percent between 1980 and 1992, while the rate for men doubled from 20 percent to 40 percent over this period.

The smoking experience in the U.S. demonstrates a common trend of smoking rates that peak earlier, as well as at a higher level, for men. The smoking rate for males in the U.S. was around 70 percent in the 1940s and 1950s. The peak for women came later, and reached only about half the rate of men, at about 34 percent in 1965. From 1965 to 1992, the total smoking rate of men declined from 51.9 percent to 28.1 percent. The rate for women declined more modestly, from 33.9 percent in 1965 to 24.6 percent in 1992.

Table II Smoking prevalence in selected countries and years

Countries	Years		Years		Years	
	Female	Male	Female	Male	Female	Male
Australia	*1945*		*1980*		*1993*	
	26	72	31	40	21	29
Bangladesh			*1980*		*1990*	
			1	67	15	60
Canada	*1965*		*1981*		*1991*	
	38	61	35	44	29	31
China			*1976*		*1984*	
			12	54	7	61
Denmark	*1970*		*1980*		*1990*	
	38	34	38	42	37	37
France	*1963*		*1976*		*1993*	
	15	57	31	60	27	40
Israel	*1972*		*1981*		*1989*	
	29	41	27	45	32	45
Italy	*1963*		*1979*		*1994*	
	8	59	18	67	26	38
Japan	*1958*		*1980*		*1994*	
	11	70	14	68	14.8	59
Republic of Korea			*1980*		*1989*	
			11	70	7	68
Singapore			*1970*		*1995*	
			4.5	42	2.7	32
Spain			*1978*		*1993*	
			17	65	25	48
Sweden	*1973*		*1983*		*1994*	
	29	37	25	27	24	22
Switzerland	*1975*		*1980*		*1992*	
	30	41	28	46	26	36
United Kingdom	*1965*		*1980*		*1994*	
	43	68	36	42	26	28
United States	*1955*		*1980*		*1993*	
	25	53	29	38	22.5	27.1
Zaire			*1980*		*1992*	
			10	20	25	40

Source: World Health Organization based on most recent available data.
www.who.ch/psa/toh/Alert/apr96/gifs/table2.gif

TOBACCO AND WOMEN'S HEALTH

Worldwide, tobacco use is estimated to cause 3 million deaths annually, with over half of these deaths occurring in developed countries. About 300,000 women in developed countries die annually from tobacco use (Chollat-Traquet, 1992) The lower death rate for women may give the misleading impression that women are less susceptible to tobacco-related illnesses. However, men and women with similar smoking characteristics are equally likely to develop smoking-related illnesses and mortality due to smoking. For women, lung cancer has surpassed breast cancer as the leading cause of cancer death for women in the U.S. in every year since 1986.

Many of the health effects unique to women are related to the antiestrogenic effect of cigarette smoking. Thus women smokers have earlier menopause and a greater risk of osteoporosis, but lower incidence of breast cancer and endometrial cancer. (U.S. Department of Health and Human Services, 1988). However, epidemiological studies have found an increased incidence of cervical cancer among women who smoke (U.S. Department of Health and Human Services, 1989). Studies show that smoking may impair the fertility of both men and women (U.S. Department of Health and Human Services, 1989).

Women who smoke during pregnancy have babies with lower birth weight. There is an increased risk of preterm delivery, spontaneous abortion, stillbirths, and neonatal deaths. Smoking during pregnancy retards fetal growth and may increase late fetal mortality and infant mortality (U.S. Department of Health and Human Services, 1989). Children of smokers have increased rates of lower respiratory tract infections and bronchitis, and exposure to cigarette smoke can aggravate asthmatic conditions. Since mothers tend to be the primary caregivers within most homes, mothers' smoking behaviour may have a greater impact than fathers' do on their children's health.

FACTORS THAT AFFECT SMOKING BEHAVIOR

This section summarises the various individual characteristics that influence whether an individual will smoke, with particular emphasis on whether these factors should have differential impact by gender.

Education

It is well known that more educated people are less likely to smoke. Education affects the ability of an individual to process information about the risks of smoking. It is also a proxy for the rate of time preference and provides information about lifetime wealth levels. Peer groups formed of persons with similar levels of education are likely to be composed of people with similar smoking habits.

Gender differences in the effect of education on smoking behaviour may arise if there are gender differences in any of the underlying factors that are proxied by education. For instance, there may be gender differences in the perception of risk. Until recently, most of the mortality caused by smoking has occurred to men, so women may underestimate the risk they face. If so, this would increase the probability that women would smoke for any given level of education. On the other hand, women tend to make uniformly safer consumer choices, controlling for individual characteristics (Hersch, 1996), which indicates they may be more risk averse in general. There may also be gender differences in the rate of time preference, which may be correlated with education. Since the life expectancy for women is greater than that of men, in anticipation of a longer life, the rate of time preference for women should be lower than that of men. This would suggest that women would be less likely to smoke than men with comparable education would. However, recent evidence suggests that the life expectancy gap is narrowing as the smoking patterns of men and women become more similar.

Physical factors

Nicotine is the drug contained in tobacco that is addictive. Men and women appear to metabolise nicotine differently, in that men excrete nicotine more rapidly than women do. Thus women may become more addicted for a given dose. Tobacco acts as both a stimulant and a sedative. There is evidence that women may be more likely to smoke when anxious or at times of stress. In addition, there is evidence that smoking is associated with depression and anxiety. Glassman *et al.* (1990) found a relation between depression and smoking, controlling for sex, education, marital status, and race. Since major depression is more common among women, women may be more likely to smoke controlling for other factors. This also implies that the proportions of smokers that are female may increase over time if such women are less likely to quit regardless of the national trend of lower smoking rates. Thus even if stress and depression have the same effect on smoking by men and women, the greater share of women with these symptoms will lead to a relatively higher smoking rate after controlling for other factors.

A number of studies have found that many individuals smoke as a means of weight control, and this reason for smoking is far more common for women. An early slogan for the American Tobacco Co. cigarette brand Lucky Strike was "Reach for a Lucky Instead of a Sweet." Indeed, individuals do seem to gain weight after quitting smoking, although the average weight gain of 3.8 kg for women and 2.8 kg for men is small (Williamson *et al.*, 1991). This small average weight gain is unlikely to have any negative consequences on health status, since smokers weigh less on average than nonsmokers otherwise the same. This use of tobacco indicates that women may be more likely to smoke than comparable men may.

Employment and occupation

Smoking by women has been associated with liberation and equality. Thus employment status, particularly in jobs not traditionally held by many women, may affect smoking behaviour differently by gender. Women employed in blue-collar occupations may be more likely to smoke. In addition, many indoor workplaces have restrictions on smoking in the workplace. Thus workers employed in white-collar occupations may be less likely to smoke. Since women are more likely to be employed in white-collar occupations, the currently lower smoking rate of women may in part reflect differences in occupation. Other employment related factors include unemployment, which is a stressful activity that may increase quantity of cigarettes smoked and make quitting harder.

Income

If health is a normal good, people with higher incomes are less likely to smoke because there is a positive income elasticity of demand for health. The share of family income earned by men is greater. If spending on cigarettes is related to who within the household earns the income, there may be differential effects by gender.

Age

The rate of time preference may decrease with age, which suggests that smokers may quit smoking as they grow older. Older people may also have more information about the risks of smoking, based perhaps on their personal health status or acquaintance with individuals who are sick or have died from smoking related illnesses. Women with their longer life expectancy should be more likely to quit smoking, while men are more likely to have personal knowledge about the health risks.

Family roles

Marital status and the presence of children have been found to affect smoking behaviour, and these factors may affect smoking behaviour differently for men and women. Divorce, separation, and widowhood are stressful events that may make quitting harder, while marriage provides social support that may make quitting easier. Although the relapse rate is high, many women smokers quit smoking while pregnant. Mothers are typically the primary care givers within a household. For this reason, mothers may quit smoking to avoid exposing their children. However, raising children is also stressful. Parents with low family incomes and parents who do not work outside of the home and are restricted in their outside activities because of child care obligations, may smoke to relieve stress or as a reward to themselves or an outlet for boredom or frustration with their lives.

Military service

There is evidence that smoking rates are higher for those who have served in the military. Since more men than women have had military service, this would lead to a higher smoking rate for men.

Sex role norms

Smoking by women has been considered inappropriate behaviour in virtually all societies.

ESTIMATES OF DEMAND ELASTICITIES BY GENDER

Data set

The data set I use in this paper is from the Current Population Survey: Tobacco Use Supplements of September 1992, January 1993, and May 1993, sponsored by the National Cancer Institute. The Current Population Survey (CPS) is a nationally representative survey of 57,000 households in each wave. Information is available monthly for persons in the household 15 years and older on a range of employment, individual, and household characteristics. Particular variables provided on the CPS used in the analysis are education, age, income, occupation, marital status, presence and ages of children, race, and gender.

In order to examine the effects of occupation and family situation on smoking status, I restrict the sample to adults age 21 to 60. I also require complete reporting on all variables used in the analysis, except for smoking as noted below. The resulting sample size consists of 47,667 individuals, with 25,075 women and 22,592 men.

Smoking data

Respondents (or their proxy) were asked whether they had smoked at least 100 cigarettes over their lifetime. Individuals who had smoked more than 100 cigarettes were then asked at what age they started smoking on a regular basis. This was followed by a question regarding whether they currently smoke every day, some days, or not at all. Respondents who report smoking every day were asked to report the number of cigarettes they smoke per day on average. Some day smokers were asked for the number of days in the past 30 days they smoked, and their average consumption on those days. The smoking question pertains to number of cigarettes smoked in the past 30 days.

Price data

Cigarette price data are from the Tax Burden on Tobacco (Tobacco Institute) for 1992 and 1993, which represent prices in November of that year. The price is a weighted average statewide price per pack, including generic cigarettes and state and federal taxes. The cigarette prices were adjusted to constant September 1992 prices by a linear interpolations between the 1992 and 1993 prices.

Family income

Annual family income is reported in 13 broad categories, topcoded at $75,000. I assign the midpoint of each category at each income level, and adjust these to constant September 1992 incomes.

Employment status

All individuals are assigned indicators values for their employment status. The categories are white-collar, blue-collar, unemployed, or not in the labour force.

Education

Education is years of education completed.

Marital status

Individuals were assigned indicator variables according to their current marital status, with the categories married, divorced, separated, widowed, and never married.

Race

The race categories are white, black, and all other races.

Children

The age of the youngest child of the respondent is assigned an indicator variable, with age categories under 3 years old, 3 to 5 years old, 6 to 13 years old, and 14 to 17 years old.

Descriptive statistics

Table III summarises smoking rates by gender, family income, and presence of children. The smoking rate for women is 24.9 percent; the rate for men is 29.1 percent. Women who smoke average 16 cigarettes per day, while men average 19.4 cigarettes per day. There is wide variation in smoking behaviour by family income and by presence of children. The smoking rates for women and men in the low-income group is 34.2 and 40.8 percent, respectively, which are well above the average. The high-income group has smoking rates well below the average, at 15.9 percent and 18.8 percent for women and men, respectively.

Despite concerns about children's exposure to smoking within the home, the presence of children in the household appears to have relatively little effect on the smoking rate for parents in low and middle income households. For instance, the smoking rate for low income women and men with children age 6 to 13 is 38.6 and 46.1 percent. In contrast, the smoking rate for parents within high-income households is substantially below their group average.

Table III Smoking rates

	Female	**Male**
Smoking rate	24.9	29.1
Cigarettes per day if smoker	16.0	19.4
By family income		
Low	34.2	40.8
Middle	24.2	28.9
High	15.9	18.8
By presence of children under 18		
All	24.2	27.2
Low family income	35.9	41.8
Middle family income	23.2	27.8
High family income	13.3	16.8
By employment status		
White collar	20.8	20.0
Not in labor force	26.7	34.3
Blue collar	31.4	34.6
Unemployed	34.4	38.5

Source: Author's calculations from the 1992-93 Current Population Survey: Tobacco Use Supplement.

Estimates of demand elasticities

Probit regression is used to estimate smoking participation equations, and OLS regression is used to estimate quantity smoked by smokers. The variables included in both sets of equations are price, family income, education, employment status and occupation group if employed, marital status, age of youngest child, and race

Table IV summarises the estimates of smoking participation and smoking consumption equations for women and men. Several points are notable. First, the price elasticities are negative, significantly different from zero, and of a similar magnitude for both men and women, with the consumption elasticities slightly larger than the participation elasticities. This suggests that an increase in tobacco prices via a tax increase will decrease both participation and consumption among smokers.

Table IV Estimates of price, income, and education elasticities

	Smoking Participation Estimates	
	Female	Male
Price elasticity	-0.33**	-0.38**
Family income elasticity	-0.25**	-0.28**
Education elasticity	-0.92**	-0.93**
Occupation (relative to not in labour force)	white-collar lower blue-collar higher unemployed higher	white-collar lower unemployed higher
Marital status (relative to married)	widowed, divorced, and separated higher	Widowed, divorced, and separated higher
Children (relative to no children under 18)	lower with children of all ages	lower with children under age 6
Race (relative to white)	Black and other non-white lower	Black lower
	Smoking Consumption Estimates for Smokers	
	Female	Male
Price elasticity	-0.56**	-0.45**
Family income elasticity	-0.05**	0.004
Education elasticity	-0.40**	-0.26**
Occupation (relative to not in labour force)	white-collar lower	white-collar lower
Marital status (relative to married)	no effect	divorced higher
Children (relative to no children under 18)	lower with children under age 3	lower with children under age 3, higher with children age 14 to 17
Race (relative to white)	Black and other non-white lower	Black and other non-white lower

** denotes coefficient is significantly different from zero at 1 percent level in one-sided tests.

Source: Author's calculations from 1992-93 Current Population Survey: Tobacco Use Supplement.

Second, higher income reduces smoking participation, and to a lesser extent, reduces consumption by smokers, consistent with a positive income elasticity of demand for health. Similarly, there is a strong inverse relation between education and smoking behaviour.

Third, occupation matters. Relative to individuals not in the labour force, white-collar workers are less likely to smoke, and of those who do smoke, they smoke less. This may be due to the higher prevalence of workplace restrictions among workers in white-collar jobs. Women in blue-collar jobs, which are not traditionally held by women, are more likely to smoke.

Fourth, individuals affected by stressful events including unemployment, divorce, separation, or death of spouse are more likely to smoke. Since very few people start smoking as adults, this suggests that stressful events reduce the likelihood that someone will quit smoking.

Fifth, smoking participation by both men and women is reduced by the presence of children. The quantity smoked is lower for those with children under age 3, however men with children age 14 to 17 smoke more than men without children under 18 or with younger children.

Sixth, blacks and other non-white people smoke less than whites, controlling for characteristics.

POLICIES OPTIONS TO REDUCE SMOKING AMONG WOMEN

Three types of public policies are available to influence smoking: raising taxes, which reduces smoking by raising the price; regulations affecting age of legal tobacco purchase and locations where smoking is permitted; and education about the risks of smoking. The findings of this paper suggest that each of policy mechanisms may help reduce smoking among both men and women, although the form and outcome of any intervention may differ by gender.

Individuals in the labour force, and particularly those in white-collar jobs, are more likely to face smoking restrictions on a daily basis. The smoking rates by employment and occupation status indicate that for both men and women, workers in white collar jobs have smoking rates considerably below the national average, followed by individuals not in the labour force, then blue collar workers, then those unemployed (who are searching for work). Women in blue-collar jobs are more likely to smoke than women not employed or employed in white-collar occupations. While rising labour force participation for women with employment in white collar jobs may have helped moderate the smoking rate for women, as more women enter non-traditional blue collar jobs, the smoking rate of women may increase.

The risks of smoking during pregnancy are highlighted in a series of Surgeon General warnings on cigarette packs. Additional outlets for information specific to women may include provision of information during medical visits for pregnancy or gynaecology. If the underlying cause of smoking is stress, depression, or weight management, treating these causes directly may be more successful.

REFERENCES

Chollat-Traquet, C. (1992), *Women and Tobacco*, World Health Organisation, Geneva.

Glassman, A.H., Helzer, J.E., Covey, L.S., Cottler, L.B., Stetner, F., Tipp, J.E. and Johnson, J. (1990), "Smoking, Smoking Cessation, and Major Depression", *Journal of the American Medical Association*, Vol. 264, pp. 1546-1549.

Hersch, J. (1996), "Smoking, Seat Belts, and Other Risky Consumer Decisions: Differences by Gender and Race", *Managerial and Decision Economics,* Vol. 17, pp. 471-81.

Tobacco Institute (1995), *The Tax Burden on Tobacco: Historical Compilation*, The Tobacco Institute, Washington, DC.

U.S. Department of Health and Human Services (1980), *The Health Consequences of Smoking for Women. A Report of the Surgeon General,* U.S. Government Printing Office, Washington, D.C.

U.S. Department of Health and Human Services (1988), *The Health Consequences of Smoking: Nicotine Addiction. A Report of the Surgeon General*, U.S. Government Printing Office, Washington, D.C.

U.S. Department of Health and Human Services (1989), *Reducing the Health Consequences of Smoking: 25 Years of Progress. A Report of the Surgeon General*, U.S. Government Printing Office, Washington, D.C.

Williamson, D.F., Madans, J., Anda, R.F., Kleinman, J.C., Giovino, G.A. and Byers, T. (1991), "Smoking Cessation and Severity of Weight Gain in a National Cohort", *New England Journal of Medicine*, Vol. 324, pp. 739-745.

14

HOW EFFECTIVE ARE TAXES IN REDUCING TOBACCO CONSUMPTION?

FRANK J. CHALOUPKA

INTRODUCTION

Governments have long taxed cigarettes and other tobacco products. Tobacco taxes have been thought to satisfy the Ramsey Rule that states that consumption taxes should be applied to goods with relatively inelastic demands so that welfare losses associated with taxation will be minimized. More recently, many countries have increased tobacco taxes to reduce tobacco use. These tax increases are partly based on efficiency grounds – the idea that tobacco users should bear the full costs of their consumption – and assume that there are social costs associated with use; thus, the tax is a "users' fee." Related to this is the use of tobacco taxes as a public health policy. The effectiveness of taxes for each these purposes depends on information concerning the impact of tobacco taxes on tobacco use. This chapter reviews this evidence.

THE IMPACT OF TOBACCO TAXES AND PRICES ON DEMAND

A fundamental principle of economics is that of the downward sloping demand curve. Many have argued that tobacco use is an exception to this law and that addictive consumption was not conducive to standard economic analysis (e.g. Elster, 1979; Winston, 1980). However, substantial economic research clearly demonstrates that the demands for cigarettes and other tobacco products respond to changes in prices and other factors. Conceptually, economists use a broad definition of price that includes not only monetary price, but also the time and other costs associated with using a product. This chapter focuses on the impact of the prices of tobacco products (which can be increased by raising taxes) on the demands for these products (see Chaloupka and Warner, forthcoming, for a discussion of the impact of other factors on demand).

Conventional studies of demand

Many studies have examined the effects of taxes and prices on cigarette demand using standard economic models of demand and diverse econometric methods applied to data from numerous, mostly developed, countries. Many have used aggregate time-series data for a single geographical unit, while others have employed pooled cross-sectional time series data; still others have used individual level data taken from surveys. Most of the price elasticity estimates for overall cigarette demand from recent studies fall within the relatively narrow range from -0.3 to -0.5.

A few recent studies have focused on developing countries (e.g. Xu, Hu and Keeler, 1998; van der Merwe, 1998). Warner (1990) argued that demand in these countries is likely to be more responsive to price than demand in affluent countries given the low incomes and relatively low cigarette consumption in poorer countries. The estimated price elasticities from these studies, about double those from developed countries, are consistent with this argument.

A growing number of studies have used data on individuals taken from large-scale surveys, producing estimated price elasticities comparable to those based on aggregate data. Because of their use of individual-level data, these studies can separately estimate the effect of price on smoking prevalence and conditional cigarette demand (e.g. Lewit and Coate, 1982; Mullahy, 1985; Wasserman *et al.*, 1991; Chaloupka and Grossman, 1996; Farrelly *et al.*, 1998; Evans and Farrelly, 1998). In general, these studies conclude that about half of the effect of price on overall demand is on smoking prevalence, with the remainder on consumption by continuing smokers. For example, Wasserman *et al.* (1991) estimated a prevalence elasticity for US adults in 1985 of -0.17 and a conditional demand elasticity of -0.09.

Evidence from the relatively new field of behavioral economics is consistent with the findings from econometric studies. These studies examine the impact of price on the self-administration of addictive substances in a laboratory setting, where price is defined as the effort required to receive one dose of a drug. One advantage of this approach is that researchers can study price changes much larger than those seen in the data used in econometric studies. The behavioral economic analyses produce elasticity estimates that are surprisingly consistent with those from econometric studies (Bickel and Madden, 1998). One particularly interesting finding from this research is that the price elasticity of demand rises as price rises.

Addiction and demand

Many recent studies have explicitly modelled the addictive nature of smoking. In these analyses, consumption is considered addictive if an increase in past consumption leads to an increase in current consumption because the marginal utility of current consumption is increased by past consumption. Empirical studies of addictive demand generally fall into two categories – those treating smokers as myopic and those treating smokers as rational. Both model the tolerance, reinforcement, and withdrawal associated with addiction. The key implication of these models for the effect of price on demand is that, because of addiction, demand will respond slowly to permanent changes in price and the long-run elasticity will exceed the short-run elasticity. The key difference is that myopic demand models assume smokers completely ignore the future consequences of their current decisions, while rational demand models assume that smokers account, at least somewhat, for the future health and other consequences of their addiction.

Myopic models of addiction developed from the literature on irreversible demand functions (those where current demand depends on all past price and income combinations), with the implication that price elasticities may differ for increases and decreases in price (e.g. Farrell, 1952). Young (1983) and Pekurinen (1989) applied this notion of asymmetric responses to cigarette price changes to data from the US and Finland, respectively. Both found that demand was almost twice as responsive to price reductions as it was to price increases. Most empirical applications of myopic models of addiction are based on the early work by Houthakker and Taylor (1966) that modelled current demand as a function of a "stock of habits" representing the depreciated sum of all past consumption. Mullahy (1985), for example, applied this approach to individual-level data from the 1979 US National Health Interview Survey (NHIS). He found strong evidence that smoking is an addictive behavior, and estimated an overall price elasticity centered on -0.47. Other approaches to estimating myopic demand models have similarly concluded that smoking is an addictive behavior and that price has a significant impact on cigarette demand (e.g. Jones, 1989; Baltagi and Levin, 1986).

Several studies have empirically modelled cigarette smoking as a rationally addictive behavior applying a theoretical model developed by Becker and Murphy (1988). In this model, addiction is reflected by adjacent complementarity, implying that current use of an addictive good will be inversely related to all past and future prices, as well as the current price, of the good. Among other things, the model predicts that addicts with higher discount rates will be more responsive to price than those with lower discount rates and that the ration of the long run to short run price elasticity will be larger as the degree of addiction rises (Becker *et al.*, 1991).

Chaloupka (1991) used individual-level data to estimate cigarette demand equations derived from the rational addiction model, finding consistent evidence that smoking was addictive and that smokers did not behave myopically. He estimated long-run price elasticities in the range from -0.27 to -0.48, about double his estimated short run price elasticities. Similarly Becker *et al.* (1994), used aggregate, state-level sales data for the US over the period 1955-1985 to estimate short and long-run price elasticities centered on -0.40 and -0.76, respectively. More recently, Douglas (1998) used hazard models to examine the determinants of smoking initiation and cessation in the context of the rational addiction model, concluding that price increases significantly raise the hazard of smoking cessation, with the duration of smoking approximately unitary elastic with respect to cigarette price.

Recent extensions to the rational addiction model address its often criticized assumption of perfect foresight and consequent lack of regret. Orphanides and Zervos (1995), for example, assumed that inexperienced users are not fully aware of the potential harm from consuming an addictive substance. Instead, their knowledge comes from observing the effects of addictive consumption on others as well as through their own experimentation. Thus, an individual who underestimates his or her potential for addiction and experiments can end up hooked to his/her regret. Suranovic *et al.* (1999), emphasized the 'quitting costs' implied by adjacent complementarity in order to explain the seeming inconsistency between smokers' stated wishes to quit and their continued smoking, as well as their use of alternative behavior modification treatments. Rather than assuming fully rational behavior, they assumed 'bounded rationality' implying that individuals choose current consumption only rather than choosing a lifetime consumption path to maximize the present value of their lifetime utility.

Empirical applications of these extensions are likely to add significantly to our understanding of the impact of price on cigarette smoking.

Subgroup differences in the price elasticity of cigarette demand

Several studies use individual level data explore the price sensitivity of population subgroups, including those defined by age, race/ethnicity, socioeconomic status, and gender. Lewit and his colleagues first examined differences in price sensitivity by age (Lewit *et al.*, 1981; Lewit and Coate, 1982). They found that demand among young adults (20-25) was more than twice as responsive to price as demand among adults and that most of the effect of price on young adult smoking was on prevalence (Lewit and Coate 1982). Similarly, Lewit *et al.* (1981), found that youths (12-17), were even more responsive to price. A decade later, however, two studies based on relatively small samples from the same survey, concluded that youths and young adults were not significantly more sensitive to price than older adults (Wasserman *et al.*, 1991; Chaloupka, 1991).

A number of recent studies based on large, nationally representative surveys for the US support the earlier findings of an inverse relationship between price elasticity and age (Chaloupka and Grossman, 1996; Chaloupka and Wechsler, 1997; Lewit *et al.*, 1997; Evans and Huang, 1998; Tauras and Chaloupka, 1999; Farrelly *et al.*, 1998). Chaloupka and Grossman (1996), for example, used data on over 110,000 youths to examine the impact of price and several tobacco control policies on youth smoking, estimating a total price elasticity of -1.31. Similarly, using 13 of the USNHIS from 1976-1993, Farrelly and his colleagues estimated a total price elasticity of demand for young adults (18-24), almost 40 percent higher than they estimated for 25 to 39 year olds and well above their estimates for older adults.

In general, researchers estimating the effect of price on smoking prevalence assume that their estimates reflect the impact of price on youth smoking initiation and adult smoking cessation. A few recent studies have directly examined the effect of price on smoking initiation. Douglas (1998) and Douglas and Hariharan (1994) applied hazard methods to retrospective data from several of the USNHIS, concluding that cigarette prices had little impact on smoking initiation. However, they note, errors-in-variables associated with both the retrospective data on initiation and the cigarette price data biased their price effects towards zero. DeCicca *et al.* (1998), addressed the same issue using data from the 1988 US National Education Longitudinal Survey and also found little impact of cigarette taxes or prices on the onset of daily smoking between eighth and twelfth grade. However, another study using these data (Dee and Evans, 1998) that treated missing data differently produced an estimated price elasticity of smoking onset of -0.63, consistent with estimated prevalence elasticities from recent studies of youth smoking based on cross-sectional data.

A few recent studies have examined differences in price sensitivity by race and ethnicity. Farrelly *et al.* (1998), for example, concluded that smoking by Hispanic and Black adults is more sensitive to price than smoking among White adults. Chaloupka and Pacula (1998) found similar differences among Black and White youths. To the extent that socioeconomic status is correlated with race/ethnicity, these findings may reflect differences in price sensitivity related to socioeconomic status. Townsend *et al.* (1994), for example, using data from the British General Household Survey, concluded that people in the lowest income groups were most responsive to price increases. Farrelly *et al.* (1998), found similar evidence in the US, estimating that the price elasticity of cigarette demand by persons at or below median family income was over 70 percent larger than for persons above the median. Chaloupka's (1991) finding that less educated persons were relatively more sensitive to price than more educated is consistent with these conclusions.

These findings have implications for the regressivity of tobacco tax increases. Over time, tobacco use has become increasingly concentrated in lower income groups and tobacco taxes paid as a share of income falls as income rises. Given this, many have argued that tobacco tax increases are highly regressive. However, the finding that lower income persons are more responsive to cigarette prices suggests that the regressivity of tobacco tax increases may be overstated. Using his recent estimates, Farrelly concludes that the relative share of federal taxes paid by low income smokers in the US would decline as price increases, reducing the apparent regressivity of tobacco taxes (Farrelly, personal communication).

Finally, several studies have examined differences in price sensitivity between men and women. In general, studies from the US have found that men are more price sensitive than women (e.g. Lewit and Coate, 1982; Farrelly *et al.*, 1998) while those from the UK conclude the opposite (e.g. Townsend *et al.*, 1994).

Price, tax, substitution, and compensating behaviour

Relatively few studies have examined the demands for other tobacco products, and fewer still have estimated cross-price effects for tobacco products. Using US survey data, Ohsfeldt *et al.* (1998), found that higher taxes on smokeless tobacco products significantly reduced the prevalence of smokeless tobacco use among adult males. Chaloupka *et al.* (1997), found similar evidence for young males. In addition, several studies have found evidence of substitution among tobacco products in response to changes in relative prices (e.g. Ohsfeldt *et al.*, 1998; Thompson and McLeod, 1976; Pekurinen, 1989).

In a recent study, Evans and Farrelly (1998) considered a different type of substitution. Using data from the 1979 and 1987 USNHIS, they examined compensating behavior by smokers in response to cigarette taxes. They constructed alternative measures of daily smoking intensity that included total cigarette consumption, total length of cigarettes consumed, tar intake, and nicotine intake. While finding that smoking prevalence and daily consumption fell with higher taxes, Evans and Farrelly concluded that continuing smokers engaged in a variety of compensating behaviors. Specifically, smokers (particularly younger smokers) in high-tax states consumed longer cigarettes and cigarettes with higher tar and nicotine content than those consumed by smokers in lower-tax states. Given this compensation, they suggested that tar and nicotine based taxes may be needed to ensure the maximum health benefits from tax increases. In practice, however, tar and nicotine based taxes have been infrequently used because of the administrative difficulties associated with them.

While compensating behavior may partially offset the health benefits of higher tobacco taxes, two recent studies that directly examined the impact of cigarette taxes on health-related outcomes show that the health benefits of higher taxes are substantial. Moore's (1996) econometric analysis of annual US state-level data on tobacco-related death rates from 1954 to 1988 concluded that higher cigarette taxes would significantly reduce smoking-related deaths. Similarly, Evans and Ringel (forthcoming), using data on approximately 10.5 million US births from 1989 to 1992, concluded that higher cigarette taxes would significantly raise birth weight.

Finally, some have suggested that higher cigarette taxes would lead to substitution of other licit or illicit substances for cigarettes. The limited empirical evidence, however, suggests the opposite. Using data for adults from several of the US National Household Surveys on Drug Abuse, Farrelly and his colleagues (1999) found that higher cigarette prices reduced the probability and frequency of alcohol and marijuana use. Chaloupka and his colleagues (1999) reached a similar conclusion for youth marijuana use.

DISCUSSION

The empirical evidence clearly indicates that higher tobacco taxes will significantly reduce cigarette smoking and other tobacco use. Several caveats, however, should be noted.

First, for tobacco tax increases to have their maximum impact on consumption, the real value of the increase must be sustained. While *ad valorem* taxes will increase with nominal prices, specific taxes will be eroded by inflation unless they are increased frequently and by sufficient amounts to maintain their real value. In the US for example, the stability of cigarette taxes was a key factor in the nearly 40 percent decline in real cigarette prices from 1971 to 1981.

Second, given the evidence on substitution among tobacco products, comparable increases in the taxes on all tobacco products are needed to maximize the health benefits of a tobacco tax hike. Moreover, given the recent study by Evans and Farrelly (1998) on the compensating behavior of smokers, differential cigarette taxes based on tar and nicotine content may be needed to maximize the health benefits of a cigarette tax increase; more research is needed, however, to determine the impact of this type of tax structure.

Third, the impact of a tobacco tax increase on consumption depends on the magnitude of the price increase that results. Several studies have considered the relationship between cigarette taxes and prices in the US. Harris (1987), for example, concluded that the doubling of the federal cigarette tax in 1983 led to a price increase that was more than twice as large as the tax increase and that could not be accounted for by increased production costs. Instead, he suggested that firms used the tax increase as a coordinating mechanism for an oligopolistic price increase. Recent research by Keeler and his colleagues, however, does not find evidence of disproportionately large price increases resulting from tax increases (e.g. Keeler *et al.*, 1996). In general, they conclude that a one-cent increase in the US federal cigarette tax would produce about a one-cent increase in cigarette prices, while a comparable increase in a state's cigarette tax would lead to a somewhat smaller increase in price given the potential for cross-border shopping.

Fourth, to the extent that organized and casual smuggling of tobacco products results from a tax increase, the effect ion consumption may be reduced. While increased tax differentials do result in some tax evasion, these differences are not the only determinant of cigarette smuggling. Joossens and Raw (1995, 1998) suggest that informal distribution networks, nonexistent or weak policies concerning cigarette smuggling, and their lack of enforcement can be as or more important determinants of smuggling than price differentials. Several options exist for limiting cigarette smuggling, including prominent tax-paid markings on all tobacco products and sizable increases in the penalties for cigarette smuggling. The Advisory Commission on Intergovernmental Relations (1985), for example, concluded that increases in the penalties for interstate cigarette smuggling in the U.S. led to substantial reductions in this activity.

Finally, earmarking tobacco taxes for tobacco control efforts, including education and prevention, media campaigns, cessation programs, and other public health efforts, as well as for crop diversification and other efforts to reduce the impact on tobacco growers can reduce some of the welfare losses associated with the tax increase and lead to larger reductions in tobacco use (Hu, Xu and Keeler, 1998).

CONCLUSIONS

The review of the literature clearly shows that the answer to the question posed in the title of this chapter is 'very effective'. Increasing cigarette and other tobacco taxes will lead to significant reductions in the use of these products, resulting from reductions in the frequency of use by continuing users, as well as reductions in the prevalence of use. Given this evidence, higher tobacco taxes are likely to be the single most effective policy option for reducing the public health toll from tobacco. When combined with other tobacco control activities, which could be funded by earmarked tobacco taxes, even larger reductions in youth and adult tobacco use could be achieved.

REFERENCES

Advisory Commission on Intergovernmental Relations (1985), *Cigarette Tax Evasion: A Second Look,* Advisory Commission on Intergovernmental Relations, Washington DC.

Baltagi, B.H. and Levin, D. (1986), "Estimating Dynamic Demand for Cigarettes Using Panel Data: The Effects of Bootlegging, Taxation, and Advertising Reconsidered", *Review of Economics and Statistics,* Vol. 68, pp. 148-155.

Becker, G.S., Grossman, M. and Murphy, K.M. (1991), "Rational Addiction and the Effect of Price on Consumption", *American Economic Review,* Vol. 81, pp. 237-241.

Becker, G.S., Grossman, M. and Murphy, K.M. (1994), "An Empirical Analysis of Cigarette Addiction", *American Economic Review,* Vol. 84, pp. 396-418.

Becker, G.S. and Murphy, K.M. (1988), "A Theory of Rational Addiction", *Journal of Political Economy,* Vol. 96, pp. 675-700.

Bickel, W.K. and Madden, G.J. (1998), *The Behavioral Economics of Smoking*, National Bureau of Economic Research, Working Paper No. 6444, Cambridge.

Chaloupka, F.J. (1991), "Rational Addictive Behavior and Cigarette Smoking", *Journal of Political Economy,* Vol. 99, pp. 722-742.

Chaloupka, F.J. and Grossman, M. (1996), *Price, Tobacco Control Policies and Youth Smoking,* National Bureau of Economic Research, Working Paper No. 5740, Cambridge.

Chaloupka, F.J. and Pacula, R.L. (1998), *An Examination of Gender and Race Differences in Youth Smoking Responsiveness to Price and Tobacco Control Policies,* National Bureau of Economic Research, Working Paper No. 6541, Cambridge.

Chaloupka, F.J., Pacula R.L., Farrelly, M.C., Johnston, L.D., and O'Malley, P.M. (1999), *Do Higher Cigarette Prices Encourage Youth to Use Marijuana?* National Bureau of Economic Research, Working Paper No. 6939, Cambridge.

Chaloupka, F.J., Tauras, J.A. and Grossman, M. (1997), "Public Policy and Youth Smokeless Tobacco Use", *Southern Economic Journal,* Vol. 64, pp. 503-516.

Chaloupka, F.J. and Warner, K.E. (forthcoming), "The Economics of Smoking", in: Newhouse, J.P. and Cuyler, A.J. (Eds), *The Handbook of Health Economics*, North Holland, New York.

Chaloupka, F.J. and Wechsler, H. (1997), "Price, Tobacco Control Policies and Smoking Among Young Adults", *Journal of Health Economics,* Vol. 16, pp. 359-373.

DeCicca, P., Kenkel, D. and Mathios, A. (1998), *Putting Out the Fires: Will Higher Cigarette Taxes Reduce Youth Smoking?* Working Paper, Department of Policy Analysis & Management, Cornell University, Ithaca.

Dee, T.S. and Evans, W.N. (1998), *A Comment on DeCicca, Kenkel, and Mathios,* Working Paper, School of Economics, Georgia Institute of Technology, Atlanta.

Douglas, S. (1998), "The Duration of the Smoking Habit", *Economic Inquiry,* Vol. 36, pp. 49-64.

Douglas, S. and Hariharan, G. (1994), "The Hazard of Starting Smoking: Estimates From a Split Population Duration Model", *Journal of Health Economics,* Vol. 13, pp. 213-230.

Elster, J. (1979), *Ulysses and the Sirens: Studies in Rationality and Irrationality,* Cambridge University Press, Cambridge.

Evans, W.N. and Farrelly, M.C. (1998), "The Compensating Behavior of Smokers: Taxes, Tar and Nicotine", *RAND Journal of Economics*, Vol. 29, pp. 578-595.

Evans, W.N. and Huang, L.X. (1998), *Cigarette Taxes and Teen Smoking: New Evidence From Panels of Repeated Cross-Sections,* Working paper, Department of Economics, University of Maryland, College Park.

Evans, W.N. and Ringel, J.S. (forthcoming), "Can Higher Cigarette Taxes Improve Birth Outcomes?" *Journal of Public Economics*.

Farrell, M.J. (1952), "Irreversible Demand Functions", *Econometrica* Vol. 20, pp. 171-186.

Farrelly, M.C., Bray J.W. and Office on Smoking and Health (1998), "Response to Increases in Cigarette Prices by Race/Ethnicity, Income, and Age Groups – United States, 1976-1993", *Morbidity and Mortality Weekly Report,* Vol. 47, pp. 605-609.

Farrelly, M.C., Bray, J.W., Zarkin, G.A., Wendling, B.W. and Pacula, R.L. (1999), *The Effects of Prices and Policies on the Demand for Marijuana: Evidence from the National Household Surveys on Drug Abuse,* National Bureau of Economic Research, Working Paper No. 6940, Cambridge.

Harris, J.E. (1987), "The 1983 Increase in the Federal Cigarette Excise Tax", in: Summers, L.H. (Ed), *Tax Policy and the Economy,* MIT Press, Cambridge, pp. 87-111.

Houthakker, H.S. and Taylor, L.D. (1966), *Consumer Demand in the United States, 1929-1970: Analyses and Projections,* Harvard University Press, Cambridge.

Hu, T-W., Xu, X., and Keeler, T.E. (1998), "Earmarked Tobacco Taxes: Lessons Learned", in: Abedian, I., van der Merwe, R., Wilkins, N. and Jha, P. (Eds), *The Economics of Tobacco Control: Towards an Optimal Policy Mix,* Applied Fiscal Research Centre, University of Cape Town, Cape Town, pp. 102-118.

Jones, A.M. (1989), "A Systems Approach to the Demand for Alcohol and Tobacco", *Bulletin of Economic Research,* Vol. 41, pp. 85-105.

Joossens, L. and Raw, M. (1995), "Smuggling and Cross Border Shopping of Tobacco in Europe", *British Medical Journal,* Vol. 310, pp. 1393-1397.

Joossens, L. and Raw, M. (1998), "Cigarette Smuggling in Europe: Who Really Benefits?", *Tobacco Control,* Vol. 7, pp. 66-71.

Keeler, T.E., Hu, T.W., Barnett, P.G., Manning, W.G. and Sung, H.Y. (1996), "Do Cigarette Producers Price-Discriminate by State? An Empirical Analysis of Local Cigarette Pricing and Taxation", *Journal of Health Economics,* Vol. 15, pp. 499-512.

Lewit, E.M. and Coate, D. (1982), "The Potential for Using Excise Taxes to Reduce Smoking", *Journal of Health Economics,* Vol. 1, pp. 121-145.

Lewit, E.M., Coate, D. and Grossman, M. (1981), "The Effects of Government Regulation on Teenage Smoking", *Journal of Law and Economics,* Vol. 24, pp. 545-569.

Lewit, E.M., Hyland, A., Kerrebrock, N. and Cummings, K.M. (1997), "Price, Public Policy and Smoking in Young People", *Tobacco Control*, Vol. 6, pp. S17-S24.

Moore, M.J. (1996), "Death and Tobacco Taxes", *RAND Journal of Economics*, Vol. 27, pp. 415-428.

Mullahy, J. (1985), *Cigarette Smoking: Habits, Health Concerns, and Heterogeneous Unobservables in a Micro-Econometric Analysis of Consumer Demand*, Ph.D. Dissertation, University of Virginia, Charlottesville.

Ohsfeldt, R.L., Boyle, R.G. and Capilouto, E.I. (1998), *Tobacco Taxes, Smoking Restrictions, and Tobacco Use,* National Bureau of Economic Research, Working Paper No. 6486, Cambridge.

Orphanides, A. and Zervos, D. (1995), "Rational Addiction with Learning and Regret", *Journal of Political Economy*, Vol. 103, pp. 739-758.

Pekurinen, M. (1989), "The Demand for Tobacco Products in Finland", *British Journal of Addiction,* Vol. 84, pp. 1183-1192.

Suranovic, S.M., Goldfarb, R.S. and Leonard, T.C. (1999), "An Economic Theory of Cigarette Addiction", *Journal of Health Economics*, Vol. 18, pp. 1-30.

Tauras, J.A. and Chaloupka, F.J. (1999), *Price, Clean Indoor Air Laws, and Cigarette Smoking: Evidence from Longitudinal Data for Young Adult,*. National Bureau of Economic Research, Working Paper No. 6937, Cambridge.

Thompson, M.E. and McLeod, I. (1976), "The Effects of Economic Variables Upon the Demand for Cigarettes in Canada", *Mathematical Scientist,* Vol. 1, pp. 121-132.

Townsend, J.L., Roderick, P. and Cooper, J. (1994), "Cigarette Smoking by Socioeconomic Group, Sex, and Age: Effects of Price, Income, and Health Publicity", *British Medical Journal,* Vol. 309, pp. 923-926.

Van der Merwe, R. (1998), "The Economics of Tobacco Control in South Africa", in: Abedian, I., Van der Merwe, R., Wilkins, N. and Jha, P. (Eds), *The Economics of Tobacco Control: Towards an Optimal Policy Mix,* Applied Fiscal Research Centre, University of Cape Town, Cape Town, pp. 251-271.

Warner, K.E. (1990), "Tobacco Taxation as Health Policy in the Third World", *American Journal of Public Health,* Vol. 80, pp. 529-531.

Wasserman, J., Manning, W.G., Newhouse, J.P. and Winkler, J.D. (1991), "The Effects of Excise Taxes and Regulations on Cigarette Smoking", *Journal of Health Economics,* Vol. 10, pp. 43-64.

Winston, G.C. (1980), "Addiction and Backsliding: A Theory of Compulsive Consumption", *Journal of Economic Behavior and Organization,* Vol. 1, pp. 295-324.

Xu, X., Hu, T-W. and Keeler, T. (1998), *Optimal Cigarette Taxation: Theory and Estimation,* Working Paper, Department of Economics, University of California, Berkeley.

Young, T. (1983), "The Demand for Cigarettes: Alternative Specifications of Fujii's Model", *Applied Economics*, Vol. 15, pp. 203-211.

Kolibri 360 GmbH
Ferdinand-Jühlke-Straße 7
99095 Erfurt, Deutschland
produktsicherheit@kolibri360.de